PNЯ252

VOLUME 46   NUMBER 4   MARCH – APRIL 2020

---------------------------------- R E P O R T S ----------------------------------

---------------------------------- P O E M S & F E A T U R E S ----------------------------------

---------------------------------- R E V I E W S ----------------------------------

Editorial

IN THE ENGLISH AUDEN, in a footnote to his 'Introduction to Poems of Freedom', Auden writes, 'during the last hundred years, artists have tended to become a social class of their own, in parallel with the general trend to specialisation, or class division, in social organisation, a tendency which has had serious consequences for both the artist and the public'. This 'social class of their own' becomes ever more specialised and defined: many individuals who identify as poets have teaching jobs in universities and colleges. Academic institutions provide relatively safe environments. They pay, protect – and some of them homogenise. If social media are a measure, poets can develop a uniform set of political and civic opinion. They police their environment tirelessly, severely. Aberrant opinion, contrary argument, are promptly slapped down. There is always the threat of cancellation.

This 'class' teaches. In some cases, they seed and replicate in their students an officious like-mindedness about poetry, about history, about theory. They can spread their concerns, prejudices and priorities. Auden, ten pages after his prescient footnote, but still writing ninety years ago, declares, 'We live in an age in which the collapse of all previous standards coincides with the perfection in technique for the centralised distribution of ideas...' It's almost as if he foresaw social media. '[S]ome kind of revolution is inevitable, and will as inevitably be imposed from above by a minority; in consequence, if the result is not to depend on the loudest voice, if the majority is to have the slightest say in the future, it must [now] be more critical than it is necessary for it to be in an epoch of straightforward development.'

To be critical, however, is to be confronted by a righteous, high-handed intransigence for which formal victory, however pyrrhic, is obligatory. A recent instance: MEAS (Measuring Equality in the Arts Sector: Literature in Ireland) published a fifteen page report entitled 'Poetry Reviews in *The Irish Times* 2013-2018' – 'with reference to gender, nationality, race and publishers. It presents data on reviewers and reviewed authors, considering what books are reviewed and who reviews them.' Though in fact it tells us nothing of the reviewing 'practices', only reporting patterns (no specific review is adduced), the facts are clear enough: more reviews of books by men than by women were published between 2013 and 2018. A MEAS report published the year before, produced by the same two researchers but not instanced in this report, demonstrated that published poetry books by men outnumbered books by women in Ireland by a ratio of 63:37, and no books by authors from ethnic minorities was mentioned – facts that might have been considered relevant here. To the Book Editor Martin Doyle's response on behalf of the *Irish Times*, published on 31 January, the researchers replied, 'We understand that it is your obligation to justify the actions of the organisation in which you are employed, but you must also understand that we are compelled to defend our own principled, unbiased, and impartial analysis of data collected with honesty and in good faith.' The *Irish Times*, among major newspapers

in these islands, has a fine record in reviewing poetry. A substantial review appears each month, and the range of books selected is wide. The 'culture of reception' is intact, and feature coverage is also given to writers and trends, Irish and otherwise. Nowadays three reviewers take turns, each contributing four substantial pieces a year. The MEAS report correctly showed that more books by men than by women had been reviewed in the period covered. But the statistical trend was shifting during that time. Had the researchers allowed us to look beyond their allotted period, they would have seen that in 2019 the ratio favoured women 60:40. They knew this, but because it was beyond the immediate parameters of their quantitative analysis they thought, being principled, unbiased and impartial, that it was unnecessary to acknowledge it. Just as they failed to acknowledge their own earlier MEAS report on gender bias in publishing. The failure to join up research, within a single programme, is regrettable. It may not be deliberate, but it looks that way, as though the researchers knew the desired result before they set out. Karl Kraus ridiculed this sort of imperative; his imagined editor tells the reporter, 'The headline is set, go find the event.'

Martin Doyle's exasperated response on behalf of the *Irish Times* (31 January) was comprehensive. His paper maintains a critical commitment to an art form that is not popular and seldom newsworthy. Seamus Heaney died in 2013, after all. Analysis, to be of any moment, having separated shes and hes, must do more if it is to be of any *value* (a risky word to use in this quantitative context). A newspaper is a particular kind of literary vehicle (academic scholars might concede). Research, to be rigorous and answerable to the medium with which it engages, might be expected to itemise what was being published in each month in question. It might give examples of titles wrongly overlooked or mis-valued, and critical reasons for naming those titles (a cultural, within a quantitative exercise). It might acknowledge which books in each month inevitably command review space in a newspaper, because of the poet – Paul Muldoon, say, Eavan Boland, Ciaran Carson, Nuala Ní Dhomhnaill. It might also ask small independent Irish publishers (a quantitative exercise) whether they supply review copies to the *Irish Times*. Not all do.

Martin Doyle had Auden in mind, too. He writes, 'W.H. Auden may not have foreseen this report's particular use of statistics when he wrote his commencement address for graduating Harvard students, "Under Which Lyre", a poem which poked fun at quantity-measuring approaches to art, and life: "Thou shalt not sit / With statisticians nor commit / A social science." However, he – and most readers of poetry – would understand the problem of reading poetry from a populist, levelling perspective, which sets aside national and international reputation and achievement, and dismisses the painstaking discussion about quality and value, alongside the obvious editorial concern with representation, which inform our critics' choices.'

Letter to the Editor

I READ WITH INTEREST the appreciation in *PNR* 251 of Glen Cavaliero as a link to the Cambridge of E.M. Forster and F.R. Leavis. No doubt there are other links – and I am one of them. In the summer of 1966 I set out, with James Fraser, a fellow undergraduate reading English at Clare, to persuade the Cambridge University Senate to accept Jim Ede's offer of Kettle's Yard and its collections as a gift to the university. As he was on Jim's list of Kettle's Yard supporters, I made an appointment to visit E.M. Forster in his rooms at King's. I found him seated on a rather spartan chaise longue with letters and envelopes from his plentiful, recently opened, morning post in pleasing confusion around him. He fed me water biscuits and eagerly signed the letter, with that quick, one movement action often used by the very old (he was 87). It seems that Forster signed the letter because he found me plausible rather than because he understood its purpose – I was so in awe of him that perhaps I didn't explain very well. (I had not only read his novels and essays but spent quite a lot of my time at Cambridge being Rickie, the protagonist of *The Longest Journey*). A week later I received a postcard from the great man, by then in Aldeburgh. A friend had written the message out for him and it was signed in the same pell-mell style. Forster wrote to tell me that he now realised what the petition I'd brought him was for and was very pleased he'd signed it as he greatly admired Jim Ede. I thought this was remarkably conscientious. It was also rather amazing that the Senate accepted the gift of Kettle's Yard a few months later.

F.R. Leavis taught Clare undergraduates in my time, first in a room at Downing, later in his house in Bulstrode Gardens. Eventually I became exasperated by his frequent diatribes against T.S. Eliot ('pusillanimous old woman', etc). If you said, 'yes, but he wrote *Four Quartets*...' Leavis would change gear and give an excellent disquisition on Eliot's merits. However, the following week the needle would get stuck in the same place, so I stopped going. However, one aspect of our sessions still impresses me. One term Leavis allowed us to set 'unseens' for him. So we assembled a few sheets of Eng. Lit. poems and prose - selecting the most abstruse examples we could find. He was able to date all of them to within some ten years of their writing. It was admirable of him to allow us to turn the tables and splendid that he performed so well.

Mark Haworth-Booth
Swimbridge, North Devon

News & Notes

Oh. Joy? · The word 'Schiller' is defined as 'a lustrous coloured reflection from certain planes in a mineral gem'. For Friedrich Schiller, the light is changing. His 'An die Freude' or 'Ode to Joy', the text set by Beethoven in his Ninth Symphony, is being replaced at a concert on 16 and 18 April at the Southbank Centre's Royal Festival Hall by Anthony Anaxagorou's 'new ode to "joy" for the 21st century' entitled 'O Human'. The press release reassures us, in the conductor Marin Alsop's words, that 'Beethoven's message of unity, tolerance and joy is as relevant today as it was in 1824. [...] Beethoven celebrated the essence of what it is to be human and what it is to be connected. We want to embrace this philosophy,' (philosophy?) 'throw the doors wide open and say: everyone owns this piece, this idea, and together, we are much stronger.' Schiller was part of the pice, of its conception and execution. No longer. Out he goes, and in comes something wholly contemporary. How is it that Beethoven himself survives? Surely it's time for a complete makeover? But no, this will be 'the biggest performance of Beethoven's 9th Symphony ever staged in the Royal Festival Hall', only it's not quite Beethoven's. It's *applied* music. 'The performance is part of global project *All Together: A Global Ode to Joy*, the brainchild of Alsop, which will see Alsop conduct Beethoven's 9th Symphony with eleven orchestras on six continents, connecting people from South Africa to China, USA to Australia throughout 2020. The UK's contribution is a celebration of youth brilliance, and Beethoven's ability to speak directly to people of all backgrounds, a sharing of joy, seen through today's eyes and heard through today's sounds; going *Beyond Beethoven*.' Same baby, different bathwater, or vice versa. '*Beyond Beethoven 9* intersperses Beethoven's blazing, radical music with new compositions by "*personable polymath*" [*The Times*] Bill Barclay (who also directs the Southbank Centre production) and a new jazz work by Benjamin Burrell (composer and musical director of the National Theatre's recent acclaimed production of *Small Island*).' Anaxagorou's replacement ode will be 'reflecting on what joy means to young people in the twenty-first century. Anaxagorou, who is also Artistic Director of Out-Spoken, a monthly poetry and music event held at London's Southbank Centre, led workshops in London secondary schools and with young refugees, asking participants what "joy" meant to them. This resulted in almost 100 poems, which Anaxagorou has used to inform his new interpretation of Schiller's famous 1785 poem.'

Frost Medal · Early in February it was announced that Toi Derricote had been awarded the Poetry Society of America's chief accolade, the Frost Medal, for her 'distinguished lifetime achievement in poetry'. Previous winners include Marianne Moore, Gwendolyn Brooks, Allen Ginsberg, Adrienne Rich, Barbara Guest, Lucille Clifton, Marilyn Nelson, Susan Howe, and, most recently, Eleanor Wilner. The citation declares, 'There are few poets who are as brave as Toi Derricotte; brave in her subject matter and brave in how she insists that even the deepest hurts must sing on the page.' Her sixth collection, *'I' New and Selected Poems*, was published in 2019. She is Professor Emerita of University of Pittsburgh and a former Chancellor of the Academy of American Poets.

T.S. Eliot Prize · Roger Robinson was awarded the 2020 T.S. Eliot Prize, a triumph too for his publisher Peepal Tree Press, which has done such service to poetry and other writing with Caribbean roots. The chair of the judges, John Burnside, said Robinson 'finds in the bitterness of everyday experience continuing evidence of "sweet, sweet life"'. The poet praised his publisher and his editor: 'They are amazing, they are amazing. It's a very small staff... but what they lack in size they have in pure attention to detail and a real love for books. Jeremy Poynting is an incredible editor.' He was brought to the publisher's attention by Kwame Dawes, now associate poetry editor, one of Robinson's poetry mentors.

Canada Calling · The Montreal International Poetry Prize returns, promising a purse of $20,000 for a poem of 40 lines or fewer. An international jury will shortlist 50 poems and the Supreme Judge Yusef Komunyakaa will chose the winner. The shortlisted poems will be anthologised in *The Global Poetry Anthology*. Further information at https://www.montrealpoetryprize.com/.

Kamau Brathwaite (1930–2020) · *John Robert Lee writes:*

> Here on the pavement lies its stump its grave its epitaph
> all in one turrible neglected jumble moment of activity
> & silence & forgetfulness –
>
> Those who come now – walk here – stumble a foot. step on
>   the trunk –
> wd nvr know that it once stood -w/tall & spread-out
>   branches leaves
> & sparkle shade & night-time dark & star-light peace &
>   some-
> times sorrow – and how it miss the Quick birds now
>
> and how the Quick birds miss it where it was –
>   Kamau Brathwaite, 'Beech tree fallen among dreams',
>   *Strange Fruit* (Peepal Tree, 2016)

Kamau Brathwaite died in Barbados on Tuesday 4 February at 89. From *Rights of Passage* (OUP, 1967), throughout his poetry and critical writing, Kamau Brathwaite gave communal voice to African peoples of the Caribbean islands and the Americas. He tested boundaries of poetic form on the printed page. *Liviticus* (House of Nehesi Publishers, 2017) and recent publications including *Strange Fruit* employed his Sycorax Video Style (SVS). Various fonts, photographs and designs were used to create word and image impressions.

Arrivants (OUP, 1973), in its early separate books, was the most radical poetry available to my generation of writers. His 'nation language', giving validation to Caribbean English, was a watershed.

With Derek Walcott, he is one of the two most influential poets of the English-speaking Caribbean. While both were concerned with Caribbean history and culture, Brathwaite's life-work probed and paid homage to the majority African inheritance. I was fortunate to know Kamau and to be in audiences during the seventies when he read, wonderfully, from his eagerly anticipated books. He was always supportive, seeking continually to encourage sustenance of a pan-Caribbean community of writers.

He has left a massive body of work, creative, historical and scholarly, that becomes a major inheritance of the Caribbean and world.

Fruitful Errata · *Nicolas Tredell writes*: George Steiner, literary critic, cultural commentator and fiction writer, died on 3 February aged 90. Steiner was a provocative figure because of the fundamental topics he addressed, his eloquent, sometimes inflated style, and his lapses in scholarship; but literary culture, especially in England, which became his uneasy home, would have been poorer without him. Steiner, born in Paris into a cultured and prosperous Viennese Jewish family, grew up speaking French, English and German and reading ancient Greek and Latin, which contributed to a lifelong fascination with the varieties of linguistic experience. His father, foreseeing the threat Hitler posed, moved the family from Paris to New York in 1940, just before the Nazi invasion, making Steiner, in the title of one of his most notable essays, 'a kind of survivor', acutely aware of his narrow escape from the fate of millions of European Jews.

Steiner studied at the universities of Chicago, Harvard and Oxford, worked as a staff writer on *The Economist*, and, at the Institute of Advanced Study in Princeton, completed his first book, *Tolstoy or Dostoevsky* (1959), a bold break with what he saw as the limitations of American New Criticism and English Leavisism. Many books followed, perhaps most notably *The Death of Tragedy* (1961), *After Babel* (1975) and *Antigones* (1984). These were more successful in their local analyses than their overall arguments, however, and Steiner, as a critic, was at his best in shorter forms. The collection *Language and Silence* (1967) remains one of his richest and most readable books; the essay form tempers eloquence with concision and a sense of intense engagement with key themes of his whole oeuvre comes through: the co-existence of culture and barbarism; the enormity of cultural decline; the urgency and difficulty of expressing in words the extremes of human experience. In contrast, later books such as *Real Presences* (1989) and *Grammars of Creation* (2001) are anti-deconstructionist polemics that slide swiftly into evasively magniloquent rhetoric. More effective is the fiction collected in *The Deeps of the Sea* (1996): the novel *The Portage to San Cristobal of A. H.* (1979), which envisages Hitler speaking powerfully in his own defence, and stories such as *Proofs* (1992), set in the twilight of Communism. But the whole body of Steiner's work satisfied the criterion he formulated in his 1990 *PNR* interview: 'it's not whether you get it right – you don't – but whether you get it wrong fruitfully'.

Nikos Kazantzakis's god-daughter · *Karen Van Dyck writes:* When Katerina Anghelaki-Rooke (1939–2020) was one year old, the celebrated writer and critic Nikos Kazantzakis stood as godfather at her baptism. When she was seventeen, he published her poem 'All Alone' in an Athenian magazine with a note saying that it was the most beautiful poem he had ever read. By her early twenties she was already an established poet. During the dictatorship (1967–74), she and a group of younger poets spearheaded a new kind of poetry that grappled with the confusion and censorship of those years. Meeting regularly with the translator Kimon Friar, they produced an anthology of six young poets, one of the first books to break the self-imposed silence initiated by the Nobel laureate poet George Seferis in response to the colonels' press laws. Linking the women poets of the previous postwar generation (Eleni Vakalo, Kiki Dimoula) to those of the generation of the '70s (Rhea Galanaki, Maria Laina, Jenny Mastoraki), Anghela-ki-Rooke stands out for the lyrical accessibility of her work. Hers is a poetry of flesh, indiscretion, and the divine all rolled into one. For Anghelaki-Rooke the body is a passageway anchoring the abstract metaphysics of myth in the rituals of everyday life. It is through the body that everything makes sense. As she once said in an interview: 'I do not distinguish the soul from the body and from all the mystery of existence... Everything I transform into poetry must first come through the body. My question is always how will the body react? To the weather, to aging, to sickness, to a storm, to love? The highest ideas, the loftiest concepts, depend on the morning cough...'

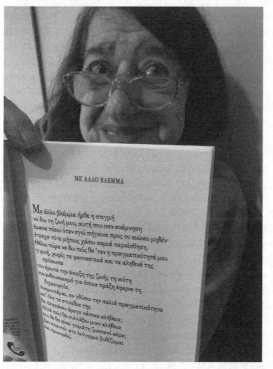

The poet holding up the poem 'With Other Eyes' for the translator last summer.

She is the author of more than twenty books of poetry and numerous translations (Pushkin, Plath, Heaney). Her own work has been translated into more than a dozen languages. She won the Greek National Poetry Prize (1985), the Academy's Poetry Prize (2000) and the National Lifetime Achievement in Literature Prize (2014). Her home was on the island of Aegina.

[*PNR* will publish new translations of the poet's work by Karen Van Dyck in the next issue.]

And from Chile... · *Neil Davidson writes*: Armando Uribe died in Santiago on the night of 22–23 January 2020, aged eighty-six. He had been widely regarded in Chile and beyond as the country's foremost living poet. He first published in 1954 and is often considered part of the Generación del 50 with poets such as Enrique Lihn and David Rosenmann-Taub, although he himself looked to Montale, Ungaretti, Pound and Browning and, in his verse forms, to the Spanish Golden Age and earlier. From first to last, his mainly short lyrics dealt with death, a Christian God he was constrained to believe in and raged against, boredom and anguish, and his own and others' baseness and folly, being saved from monotony by humour and an inexhaustible capacity for contemptuous self-exposure. He was a lawyer who rose to become director general of the diplomatic corps and spent the years before Allende's election in Washington, distilling what he learned there after the coup in a political tract, *The Black Book of American Intervention in Chile*, which was translated into numerous languages. Returning from exile in 1989, he was debarred from positions of influence by his contempt for everyone he considered to have compromised with and perpetuated the dictatorship – almost the entire political and business class. 'Cloistering' himself in his home to await death, he discovered a new career as an oracle and consummate entertainer whose unsparing views on all topics were eagerly sought: a position he retained until the end. I shall remember him as the person who, in his books and the few conversations I was able to have with him, did more than anyone to make me aware of the obstinate survival beneath a homogenised surface of an older Chile of great beauty and distinction.

Roddy Lumsden is Dead (2001) · And now (2020) he really is dead, fulfilling that premature prophesy, though he was only 53 when the actual end came in January. His relatively short publishing life began in 1997 with *Yeah Yeah* and ended with his T.S. Eliot Prize shortlisted final collection *So Glad I'm Me* (2017). His *Guardian* obituarist Neil Cooper wrote, 'As a teacher, editor, mentor and champion of younger writers, Lumsden's influence on a new generation of British poets is immeasurable. He nurtured hundreds of writers, both for the generation-defining anthology, *Identity Parade: New British & Irish Poets* (2010) and beyond. He also channelled his astonishing facility for obscure words and facts into Vitamin Q: a temple of trivia lists and curious words (2004).'

At this year's T.S. Eliot Awards his influence was acknowledged by Ian McMillan: 'Many people here will owe the way they write to Roddy Lumsden.'

David Wright · To celebrate 100 years since the birth of the poet David Wright, a group of friends and admirers will gather to read a selection of poems from 7 p.m. to 8 p.m. on Friday 29 May 2020 at the Freemasons' Arms, 81–82 Long Acre, Covent Garden, London WC2E 9NG. Admission is free. A pay bar is available.

'Listen, Pops': Desdemona Speaking

Vahni Capildeo

If you think of Shakespearean characters who refuse to die, masculine heroes might come to mind. In *Antony and Cleopatra*, Mark Antony gloriously drags out his unsoldierly demise. In *Hamlet*, the prince's procrastination, ostensibly a refusal to kill the king (since adapting to court life is clearly not an option for him) is also a refusal to be either killed or crowned. It is, however, the women who are dramatically addicted to being alive. The comedies spring to mind, with their pretend deaths: the fainting Hero in *Much Ado About Nothing*; in *A Winter's Tale*, the long-gone Hermione who plays her own statue that disconcertingly is warm to the touch. These women have been 'killed' by bad words; the suspicion cast on them by men. Their resurrection, absurd and fabulous at plot level, brings serious embodiment as well as wondering laughter to the stage. It is a promise of new life, if and when faith can be renewed. That is a lot to carry.

Strangely, it is a woman in a tragedy who shows the most terrible vitality of all, yet tends to be remembered as a broken doll: Desdemona; and what she has to carry, in language, is even more than the women of the comedies. When the multitalented Dan Burley, as a musician, famously picked up on and compiled Harlem slang, he also wrote his own versions of well-known dramas, including *Othello*, 'As Conceived in Harlem Jive'. This is now available in Thomas Aiello's edition, *Dan Burley's Jive* (Cornell University Press, 2009), which comprises *Original Handbook of Harlem Jive* (1944) with his *Diggeth Thou?* (1959). It is easy to delight wildly and precisely in Burley's language, but it would be as reductive to view him as parodying Shakespeare, as it would be po-faced to analyze him as making a creative translation of the English Bard.

Notably, like Verdi and Boito before him when they refashioned *Othello* into the opera *Otello*, losing Venice to gain bonfires, ballet, the devil in music, and prayers, Burley seems to think Desdemona deserves more lines; that she was not given enough to say for herself before, or maybe that she is a character whose nature it is to be unstoppable. His playlet is a version of Shakespeare's super-compressed Act V, scene ii which goes on for pages, long after henpecked Othello says 'Don't beat up thy chops, so much, chick!' Burley's Othello is determined to 'Stash the spark, and then, I say, Stash the spark!' His Desdemona is as gabby in the bedchamber as she was when on the docks of Shakespeare's Cyprus, asking her husband: 'What are thou putting down; And, what is thy play?' Jive Desdemona tries to survive, and to thrive: she invites Othello to sleep with her and to *listen to her*, in modes both sensual/sexual and domestic/nurturing: 'Wilt thou stash thy fine brown frame on this righteous softy with me, ole man, and let me soft gumbeat thee a bedtime fable?' Elements of the whole play zoom, smoulder and sparkle through the flashback and allusion of established couple chat, as we learn that 'the stud, Cassio' has fallen victim to 'that square, Iago' who 'is down with the action'.

Stop a moment and consider: how many times does Desdemona refuse to die, in Shakespeare's *Othello*? She asks for time to say 'one prayer'. Othello tells her 'too late'. The seasoned combatant, Othello, fails to snuff his delicate young wife on the first go. As Desdemona's attendant Emilia calls to be let into the bedchamber, Othello asks himself, or asks his expiring wife: 'Not dead? not yet quite dead?' He pronounces 'She's dead', before letting in Emilia, who has continued to raise a ruckus. Emilia comes in and announces the death of young Roderigo at the hand of Othello's preferred lieutenant, Cassio. Desdemona comes back to life sufficiently to denounce the injustice: 'O, falsely, falsely murder'd!' Unavoidably, this announces her own murder, botched murder, or murder-in-progress.

She must be living for something. Is it to accuse Othello? No. She tells Emilia her own death is 'guiltless', which has a double meaning. Yes, the adjective may serve as an assertion of Desdemona's innocence, in a play where a competitive, military and multicultural setting turns up the heat on characters to guard or attack reputations by living out virtue, or its loss, as a performance. Yet, living long enough to answer Emilia's question about the murderer's identity, Desdemona offers a riddle: 'Nobody; I myself'. She dies remembering her 'kind lord'.

The point here is hardly that Desdemona is covering for or enabling an abuser, thus dying a liar, as Othello does not hesitate to call her. While Burley's Desdemona is more fun, as she tries to tough it out and prolong a conflict into resolution, i.e. move through tragedy into comedy, Shakespeare's Othello and Desdemona have insane ambition. They attempt a vast linguistic challenge: to follow a Petrarchan courtship with a thoroughly Christian marriage. In the language of the play, this means making the conventional courtly exchange of epithets such as 'fair warrior' and 'dear' carry the weight of a mutual and unbreakable oneness. It means the tingle and tinsel of beautiful utterances made by compelling actors has to accompany, while counting for less than, the substantial unity implied and created by the exchange. Style and substance are both at one and at odds.

Iago's mirroring or corrupting of his companions', especially Othello's, speech habits receives popular attention for its vicious and seductive cleverness, notably in Verdi's opera where Iago launches audibly exact yet toxic echoes of others' song. Just as fascinating, whatever one's views, is how the religious and conjugal oneness desired by the idealistic and unhappy pair equally could be traced at length in their sharing and borrowing of lexis and syntax, and not least their turn-taking. They often choose to give each other voice rather than speak, for example near the beginning when Desdemona objects volubly to the Venetian officials' suggestion that she stay in Cyprus, and Othello quietly agrees with her. He stands aside in order to stand with, in a speaking-after which is humbler and more committed than a speaking-for, significantly different from a superior holding silence then giving approval.

Desdemona therefore finally insists on dying in a state of identification with Othello. She remains purely married, purely in language, even if the marriage has ended with their lives. Othello's morbid running of checks to see if she is still alive is thus as much dialogue as soliloquy; he, too, remains involved, though fallen. What framework of understanding, if any, can we find for two articulate lovers who lead each other to such a place? The idea of active consent in *Othello* will be explored in an essay to follow.

Cavalier Ballads

William Poulos

It must be a tough life, a cavalier's. Imagine losing your land and fighting for your king only to have your name synonymous with an intemperate lifestyle and a rather small, affectionate class of dog – not, one must admit, a fitting reward for your efforts. Besides the ridicule of posterity, you would have had to endure the ingratitude of your peers: upon the Restoration, twelve seats in Charles II's new Privy Council were given to Cromwellians. Parliament did little to redress Cavaliers' lost land, which was confiscated or sold by the Interregnum authorities who convicted them of treason. The Cavaliers were salty about it.

While the Puritans spread their message via sermons, the Cavaliers spread their resentment through ballads, songs, and litanies. The ballad 'A Cavalier's Complaint', printed in 1661, a year after the Restoration, records the feelings of a man who returns to court hoping to see his fellow Cavaliers but is disappointed:

> S'life, of so many Noble Sparkes,
> Who, on their Bodies, bear the Markes
> Of their Integritie,
> And suffer'd Ruine of Estate;
> It was my damn'd unhappy Fate,
> That I not One could see...
> But, truly, There are swarmes of Those,
> Who lately were our chiefest Foes,
> Of Pantaloons and Muffes;
> Whilst the Old rusty Cavaleer
> Retires, or dares not once appear
> For want of Coyne, and Cuffes.

The last three lines provide an image of a Cavalier different from the one most people have: he bears scars gained in war; the adjective 'rusty' hints at the old armour he might have used fighting for the King. He is not the laughing Cavalier of Frans Hal's painting; he is not dressed in lace or embroidery. He doesn't even have cuffs. It's a tough life, a cavalier's.

The most famous ballad-writer from this period is probably Alexander Brome, who in fact wasn't a courtier but a lawyer. I say 'famous', but really, he's known only to a few academics: a cruel fate, considering that his contemporaries obviously liked him. In the few years after the Restoration he published three editions of his *Songs and other Poems* and in 1675 Edward Philips said that 'his name cannot chuse but be immortal'. Brome's name may not have chosen to be dead, but dead it is. It's a tough life, a cavalier's.

His name, though, has many ballads attributed to it. He probably didn't write them all, but his contemporaries described him as an 'English Anacreon', and much of his work is in the jokey, drinking-song style you might expect from a 'Cavalier' poet. He denigrated his own work as 'harmless lines', written to amuse himself and his close friends, but there's a sadness and a complexity to some of it which belies his description. In 'The Royalist' he uses something very close to a Metaphysical conceit to contrast the disorder of the world with an ever-renewing cosmic order created by drink:

> Our selves will be a Zodiack,
> And every mouth shall be a sign.
> Me thinks the Travels of the glasse,
> Are circular like *Plato's* year,
> Where every thing is as it was;
> Let's tipple round; and so 'tis here.

The red mouths, or possibly the faces flushed with drink, become stars in the boozy constellations which move around after the alcohol has taken hold. There is an element of the 'nothing's going well so let's have a drink' sentiment here, but drink, especially strong drink, had Cavalier associations: during the Interregnum, a grain shortage, an excise on alcohol, and new, strictly enforced price mandates decreased the production strong beer and ale. Many Cavalier authors echoed public sentiment by scorning Parliament for its policies. In 1649 an anonymous pamphlet called *A Curse against Parliament Ale* rebuked Parliament for practically eliminating strong ale, 'the nourisher of blood'. Your king sent into exile and nothing to console you except weak drink: it must have been a tough life, a cavalier's.

Brome's ballad 'The Cavalier' shows us the sadder side the Cavaliers, proving that his work was more than 'harmless lines':

> We have ventur'd our estates,
> And our liberties and lives,
> For our Master and his mates,
> And been toss'd by cruel fates...

This might lack poetic invention, but here Brome marks the movement away from Metaphysical conceits towards the clarity of writers such as Denham and Dryden. More importantly, some of 'The Cavalier' is quite moving:

> We have laid all at stake
> For his Majesty's sake,
> We have fought, we have paid,
> We've been sold and betray'd...

In other poems, Brome elegises his friends and praises them for their constancy. Like them, he never supported the Cromwellian or Interregnum governments. Another Cavalier poet, Richard Lovelace, languished in prison and, according to legend, died in poverty. His poems, though, are in almost every poetry anthology you can find. Brome had a successful legal career and died in his home six years after the Restoration. You can't find his poems anywhere. It's a tough life, a cavalier's.

A New Source for Keats's 'Nightingale'

John Clegg

Musarum deliciæ: or, The Muses recreation, by the Cavalier poet Sir John Mennis (with contributions from James Smith), was first published in 1656, and ran to a few editions. It was not reprinted during the eighteenth century. In 1817, E. Dubois oversaw a new edition – by subscription only, since it is intermittently a very obscene collection, and incorporating two other mid-seventeenth-century volumes, *Wit Restor'd* and *Wit's Recreation*. It is in this edition that I believe Keats lighted upon Mennis's poem 'The Nightingale', sometime before beginning his Ode.

Where exactly he lighted on the book is a difficult question. It is mentioned in an interesting-sounding footnote in Percy's *Reliques of Ancient English Poetry*, which Keats had certainly read. Alternatively, Leigh Hunt had a long association with Epsom – about which Mennis had written his most famous poem – and discussed its cavalier history in *The Companion* ('A Walk from Dulwich to Brockham'). This was many years after Keats's nightingale; is it possible, all the same, that Hunt's interest in Epsom had begun earlier, that he was one of Dubois' 150 subscribers, and that Keats had found *Musarum deliciæ* in Hunt's Hampstead library? Mennis's style, I think, would not have repelled Keats; I take it that what he objected to in Byron was the superiority of tone, the innate sneer, which he might have found in many Cavalier lyricists but not in Mennis. Mennis's humour is much closer to Keats's 'Cap and Bells', or the squib beginning 'Give me women, wine, and snuff'; much closer to Rabelais than to Wilmot.

'My limbs were weary, and my head oppressed / With drowsiness' begins 'The Nightingale'. Keats: 'My heart aches, and a drowsy numbness pains / My sense'. In the manuscript of the poem (held at the Fitzwilliam Museum), Keats considered and then deleted 'fearful' for 'drowsy'; 'fear-distracted' appears in 'The Nightingale' a few lines later. Over the next four lines, both poems describe an experience of half-sleep; both, in their sixth lines, reject a possible cause of their condition. ('Tis not through envy of thy happy lot.' / 'No fear-distracted thoughts, my slumbers broke.') Here the poems diverge, 'The Nightingale' into dull classical allusions, Keats into the most astonishing verse of the nineteenth century. But both poems end with the poet in the same condition, suspended between sleep and waking: 'Methought I lay content, though not at rest' is the line which closes Mennis's 'The Nightingale', perhaps the strongest line in the poem, reiterating subtly the opening rhyme. 'Oppressed // ... at rest' is a rhyme-pair, in fact, that summarises the concerns of both poems: concerns which, of course, are worked through far more and expressed far more lastingly by Keats than Mennis. 'Fled is that music: – Do I wake or sleep?'

A further parallel between the poems is solely on the level of rhyme. A lot of readers have found Keats's 'deceiving elf' in the final stanza of 'Ode to a Nightingale' jarring; Mennis has 'Sleep's foe, the Flea, that proud insulting Elf'. In both cases, the only justification for 'elf' is that there aren't many other words which rhyme with 'self'. And, perhaps, both elves need to be qualified with adjectives because they are needed to point out the particular connotations of the metaphor. (I hadn't noticed until I started thinking about it now that there's an ambiguity in Keats's elf deceits: is the metaphor that Fancy can deceive or cheat like an elf, but can't do it very skilfully? – or that Fancy is an elf which is deceitful about how much it can cheat?)

Other connections are more tenuous. Both poems include metaphors of faeryland:

> ... wheresoe're she [the nightingale] flyes
> The Grovy Satyr, and the Faery hyes
> Afore her perch, to dance their Roundelayes...

which might have vaguely suggested Keats's Queen-Moon on her throne, 'Cluster'd around by all her starry Fays'. But the central points of connection are the first few lines of each poem, the insulting / deceiving elf, and the half-sleeping half-waking conclusions.

Robert Gittings traced many of the images in Keats's ode to his reading of the medieval verse allegory 'The Flower and the Leaf', in the original (at that time erroneously attributed to Chaucer) in 1817, and then in early summer 1819 in a reworking by Dryden. These two nightingale sources do not overlap at all in Keats's finished poem; the images which he drew from Dryden appear predominantly in the middle stanzas, with which 'The Nightingale' of 1656 has nothing to do. Likewise, the machinery borrowed from Robert Burton has nothing to do with the passages I suggest derive from Mennis. (I find my parallels, incidentally, more convincing than either; what the Gittings suggestions have going for them is the proof that Keats had definitely read the source material. But Dryden's 'Where stood the Eglantine with lawrel twin'd' seems to me not especially close to Keats's 'White hawthorn, and the pastoral eglantine', which is the strongest of the parallels Gittings points out.)

None of this, obviously, has any bearing on how we should approach 'Ode to a Nightingale' as readers; it might contribute something to our knowledge of Keats's reading. But even if all the parallels are coincidence, as they may well be, I don't think Keats would object to being linked with Mennis. Mennis's other claim to fame is as the man who once met Shakespeare's father, recorded in Thomas Plume's marginal annotation: 'His Father was a Glover; Sir John Mennis saw once his old Father in his shop a merry Cheekd old man that said Will was a good Honest Fellow, but he durst have crackt a jeast with him at any time.' Mennis a true word spoken in jest.

Letter from Wales

Sam Adams

My grandfather's lamp, suspended by its hook, hung from a nail driven high into the wall in our outside lavatory. It was so familiar a sight for me as a child that I ceased to notice it. When the house in Gilfach Goch was cleared ahead of sale it was one of the items I bore away. Even then I gave it little attention. Many years passed before its significance and worth dawned upon me. I treasure it now as a twofold connection with the past, one personal, as an object contributing to the story of my family, the other general, as an artefact recovered from the history of the South Wales coalfield.

It is an overman's lamp, somewhat smaller than those one sometimes sees in bric-a-brac shops, and made entirely of brass rather than the more usual steel and brass. It is intact, even to the wick, after a hundred years or so, though dented (wounded if you like). Sometime during its working life a heavy weight has fallen on it with force enough to fracture the circular boss at the top and drive it downwards a millimetre or two. The broken metal has been soldered in the blacksmith's shop (every colliery had a blacksmith's shop), but this scarred lid and the ring of perforations immediately below it remain buckled.

At intervals, I have taken a rag and a tin of Brasso and brought up the shine on it, but over the years an unsightly white deposit has built up in inaccessible folds and joints. Recently I tried submerging the lamp in a solution of a new kind of cleaner. It was not a complete success as traces of Brasso remain, but the brass looks refreshed, and, much to my surprise, when I emptied the bowl I found at its base a layer of the finest coal dust somehow displaced from recesses in the interior of the lamp. There it was; the very same black death that silted the lungs of my grandfather and snatched him away from us so shockingly in middle age, no more than a week after I was born. That is why I bear his name: Samuel.

As overman, my grandfather was responsible for the safe and productive effort of colliers underground in a section of the mine. His brass lamp was a symbol of office. He also carried a cleft stick which allowed him to lift the lamp by its hook to examine the roof of a heading where men were at work and test for the presence of firedamp, the flammable gas readily ignited by a naked flame or even a chance spark from a pick striking rock. The damage to the top of the lamp might have been caused by thrusting it against a low roof, or perhaps when a stone fell on it. 'Stone' is a characteristic understatement of the mining industry: a stone might weigh several hundredweight. Mining was never a safe occupation. I was told that in his tours of the coalface my grandfather would sing hymns (he and his wife were staunch Salvationists), so that men on the shift would know of his approach and would be found busily and carefully at work.

My grandfather's grandfather, William, from the old mining area of Newhall, Derbyshire, and his wife Rachel, a Breconshire girl from Llangynidr, settled in Abersychan, in the 1820s and, apart from brief forays to try their luck elsewhere in South Wales, remained there until 1851 and beyond. What brought them to that place? The simple answer is the likelihood of a steady living, for there was a concentration of industry nearby. The Afon Llwyd ('grey river', a name replete with significance for anyone familiar with a mining area) rises on Mynydd Coety overlooking Blaenavon and winds some thirteen miles through Abersychan and Pontypool down to its confluence with the Usk at Caerleon, about half a mile from where I sit. It is one of those curious geographical coincidences, the sort that shouldn't be pressed too far, but nevertheless gives me a sense of connection.

The upper reaches of this Monmouthshire valley, and the six miles between Blaenavon and Pontypool, were the setting of some of the earliest manifestations of the Industrial Revolution in Wales – before the great days of Merthyr and the Rhondda. In 1840, works in that stretch produced and transported by canal fifteen thousand tons of iron. Coal was mined alongside ironstone and there was, within a short distance, a choice of location and heavy labour for men and women, and their young children if they were prepared to risk them. In 1842, a government commission into the employment of children found there were 185 children under the age of thirteen employed at the Blaenavon ironworks. The furnace manager said they sometimes got burned 'but not very bad'. Search the internet for 'Llanerch Colliery, Abersychan' and you will certainly come across a photograph of the pit – engine house, stacks, pithead winding-gear – and, assembled in the middle ground, a crowd of black-suited men. It must have been taken soon after 6 February 1890. Despite warning from an inspector of mines, in the previous December the mine manager had declared it safe to work the pit with naked lights. On that fateful day in February a massive gas explosion killed 176 men and boys. Long before then my immediate Adams kin had moved on, into Glamorganshire. The role of overman and the safety lamp my grandfather carried were intended to prevent such disasters. They didn't, of course (think of Senghenydd, 14 October 1913, where 439 were killed), though the existence of precautionary measures probably meant there were far fewer than would otherwise have been the case.

There are substantial remains of colliery and ironworks and terraced workers' cottages in Abersychan, but a more complete experience of the industrial past has been preserved at Blaenavon (a World Heritage site, three miles or so further up the valley), first in the ironworks – including furnaces, foundry and cast house, and via an open square of restored workers' cottages. The 'truck shop', among the cottages was the company store for groceries and all other necessities. No alternative existed: workers were paid in tokens that had value only in that shop, which in the 1830s was providing one-tenth of the company's profits. Less than a mile off, 'Big Pit' provides the faintest taste of a working coal mine, which it was indeed until 1980. A friend from the Rhondda Fach tells how, as a teenager, he was taken down the local pit by his father on a Sunday morning when only repair teams were busy underground. It was not a pleasant experience. 'If you don't work in school, this is what you'll get', his father told him. He became a scientist and successful businessman. Late last year we visited Big Pit together. Mining safety regulations still apply: you leave watches and mobile phones behind before descending 300 feet in the cage, wearing a hard hat and safety lamp powered by an eleven-pound battery on a belt around your waist. No dust now, none of the incessant clamour of coal-cutter, shot-firing, picks and shovels, men's voices, journeys of drams. The stables are there but not the horses that hauled the drams, empty to the miner's stalls and full to the cage waiting at the bottom of the pit. There, too, at the end of the shift the weary, coal-grimed men assembled for the haul to the surface and the blessing of fresh air.

From the Journals

R. F. LANGLEY

from a long continuous entry begun on 23 and continued on 24 and 25 August 1974

(A summer holiday with Barbara and Ruth, aged six months, in Glebe Cottage, Spexhall, near Halesworth, Suffolk, shared with Kate, Nigel and one year old Daniel Wheale, involving expeditions to look at medieval Suffolk churches, with pauses and picnics in the countryside in between)

Gipsywort in the choked ditch by the row of cottages behind Bedingfield... tall, erect, square hard-stemmed, with pairs of yellow-green deep-notched stems , graduated perfectly in size, opposite, the next pair turned through ninety degrees, each pair springing from a small cushion of spikes and smallest white flowers in the upper cushions. A plant so regular and designed effectively as to be artificial if it were not rankly natural. Scentless. A visual articulation. An elegant gypsy, Lycopus europaeus, lanceolate, staged blades, hafted, toothed, whorled like shaft decoration. By fresh water.

The church door, remarkable only for the simplest double hammerbeam ever, no tracery, no decorated wall plates, just the structure in plain wood so what virtue it has shows. After Fressingfield, where it rained, but the square nave was light, the pale oak of the benches answering that of the roof equally, nowhere else was of note, though Bedfield was swathed in heavy-duty polythene, a curtain of it closing off the chancel, all benches, floor and font smothered, dead myxymatosis rabbit at the door, loud ducks on the stirred brown pond, a foreign pheasant rushing across the churchyard, mint by a pool, puddles, smeared mud... and Ubbeston locked, door handles removed, mere tracks stamped narrowly to its walls from the collapsed gate, the inside, seen through removed panes, spattered with droppings like a bird of prey's nest, ladders in there, woodwork askew, porch wall slime green. It is joining the Roman building that was on that tump.

So now we have worked that wide flat plateau with the A1120 at its south, cornered by Halesworth and Eye at its top. Upland feel. Hedgeless roads with buff grass fringes or choked ditches. A rim of rain-blue trees, elm or oak, always collecting round the horizon, and always scattered

houses, moated farms, pantile roofs smouldering orange, bright white walls, odd water towers in grey concrete on stilts, towers in clumped woods, no black thunderbugs at this tiom eof the year, wide skies full of varied cloud, cornfields, cabbages, some sweetcorn, beans, brown -red turned earth on huge fields, small parties of gulls on the roads, rising. Willow often, full-sized trees white-blue, brightening, blowing, double swerves on the roads, flints worn brown and grey, always a new flower, rooks flap, a squirrel crosses, rabbits, more typically moorhen with parties of young.

The gems are Dennington, Worlingworth, Badingham. Debenham disappoints, a barn with bits in it. Wilby is too spruced and badly shaped, Athelington too, renovated outside and suspect even down to its shrunken bench-ends, where only Dennington and Fressingfield have the full spinning globes. Framlingham popular and ornate.

Tuesday 25.
Ruth sat up today for the first time, on the floor of the middle room downstairs , for a quarter of an hour. Put to use at once as she feeds on the verge at Gislingham.

Fast weather today, and very high winds last night which blew a milk bottle off the stand by the door and smashed it, broke down an elder sapling in the corner between the kitchen and the bathroom extension, and left showers of horsc chestnuts under trees in the lanes. Clouds pass in steady hurry, strips of light blue, distant fields of ice-white small knobbed cumulus, whipped grey flather low, with surprisingly vertical edges, or heavy cumulo-nimbus in the middle distance with falling rain in long diagonal shafting beneath. Watch the rain crossing the country. By the time we get to Gislingham, however, the sun is out though the wind is still gusty and no conditions last long. The sunlight is washed gold while it is here. Key from the Mill Road Farm as before. The decay seems paused at the most precious point. Colour and surface here as nowhere else, and with great subtlety and with cheeriness in this morning's brisk weather.

(This description of Gislingham church will be continued in the next issue.)

edited by Barbara Langley

Warm Ocean and other poems

BILL MANHIRE

Warm Ocean

Someone says lonely let's go for a stroll
someone says not now
someone says it was never about the money
someone says what then
someone says a few basic rules
anger desire compassion
anger desire compassion
and then there's a great silence
in which we all go for a stroll
clifftop ocean a few swimmers far below

Old women are swimming in the ocean
there's classical music going on
so many heads bobbing and nodding
where is my lover, where is my lover
the women cry, bobbing and nodding
and they all take up the cry
and violins you know
where is my lover, where is my lover
and now the small girl is asleep

Three old men late afternoon
last ones left in the water
come on admiral! says one
but it's not clear which one
or who to – maybe us?
they want us to watch them don't they   no
they want us to go away   no
they want us to set a net
and spend our last days hauling in

Long bench where men sat once
stubborn wood
old driftwood trunk
before the vows and boasts
before the oars demanding water
before the killings
before the killings and the weepings
before the poet's song
before the later tales about the killings
the ones they made from fish and cigarettes

Long stretch of wood with nothing there
except you know patches of drifting grain
maybe a piece of cloud maybe a tiny stream
a few books
and on the stream-bed the stones knocking together
you can hear them *clock*
when you turn off the noise of the world
there they are going *clock cluck*
clock cluck clock like time itself

a busy creature deep below the surface
each time you put your ear to the timber

Well anyway I think I prefer the inland forest
birds with their dings and dongs and dusky wings
making some beauty
making all of us shiver
even when crying there's a sail a sail
telling us over and over yes and forever
that the ghost can't stand the graveyard

Ancient man clad in bells
he jumps and terrifies the children
the adults too clang clang
we wonder a bit why we came here
something on the radio perhaps
or maybe the kids had heard it somewhere
anyway here we are yelling at him you fucking
fucking cunt we yell and why
have you come here clanger-cunt! as he runs
into the forest same old forest
followed by all our women
chirping and cheeping and chasing
off once again to hide among the birds

The where-am-I bird is singing again
deep in the woods the bush the forest
people lost in the undergrowth
swearing at each other as you do
as you mostly don't when you're hunting
and now the where-am-I bird
is reshining its song
up-in-the-sky   up-in-the-sky
everyone looking up high now of course
taking aim and lost for an answer
gone-now-for-good
and now just to settle everything down
the bagarup bird is squawking again
on the general's desk by the caged canary
by the potted daisy oh there's the telephone

The god rises up out of the river
so we make the temple on the riverbank
big white flowers like plates we might eat from
then the bodies the blindfolds the blur
and rain puzzled by its own prosperity
one and two and three and others
blessing the coming and the going
the generous bodies hauled high
as blood weeps out of eyes and ankles
the shame and plaque and tangle

so the world will be better now god help us
now that the god is finally helping

The huge man carries his tiny candle
he stumbles forward picking people up
then yes tossing them aside
his hand is huge, all handle
he gasps behind his tongue behind his smile
walks into the water *apparently*
and soon he is remote like a ripple
like something sighing
like the troubled echo of a sigh
and someone comes up to us and says
really to anyone who'll listen
how could he come along and leave like that
not even buying a ticket

Like possible footprints on the ocean floor
possibly there possibly not
that's the way her memory paces
to and fro to and fro
and who exactly are you anyway
to and fro with your talk of a kiss gone missing
and your all in all and your wherewithal
and all of those things that aren't material
that's not what we want from an answer
no we never wanted anything like that
maybe snow melting and frost in a field
maybe sand that shuffles aside when she whispers

Don't play the music don't play the music
says the man
who walks around town saying
over and over don't play the music
all songs being made
as we know from things that hurt
ice that melts flames that fall from the sky
yes all of that and more
                         all of that and more
and the father goes on singing
long after his daughter leaves the church

Last night in the world's last city
no one much about
though here you are again turning a corner
and there are the abandoned cruise ships
just imagine
no one lives there now
                      and here you are again
stepping around small fires
it's all moonlight and shipwrecks these days
kids and parents jumping off the wharf
the orchestra breaking up the ballroom
to make warm ocean anyone could swim in

Someone Was Burning the Forest

We did not know why the child was crying,
nor why he stood bare-shouldered at the window.
How had he come by those skimpy feathers?
The mother had fallen from the tower
a moment after she began to answer. I looked around
and there were many towers, also other bodies.
Now I was on the ground myself. I could hear
the child but no longer see him. Perhaps
he was still aloft. The towers were dissolving
yet surely there were trees. It was dark now
but I knew there must be many bodies.
I would need to climb to see where we might go.

The Kaffir Lime is Having a Bad Day

I was made of clusters.
I functioned in secret ways.
I called out in a voice
I did not recognise as my own.
That was one way to do it.

~~You learn not to trust people.~~
~~You want the whole thing to finish.~~

I went through the door.
No colour in the great outdoors,
just the cold attacking wind.
The sparrow spread its tiny wings.
Oh it was opening up the sky.

Wow

Big brother
says also but the baby always says wow,
though soon enough she too is saying also
and listening to her father say later,
and to the way her mother sighs and says
now would also be a very good time.

The ghost would love to say also
but cannot actually say anything
aside from that quiet whooshing sound,
and now there are babies everywhere
all saying wow for a time, and the children grow,
and the children grow, and the wife
goes off for a bit of a break
and never comes back. Also the lawn gets away on him.
One thing after another.

Now the old fellow wants his bed sheets changed.
No one the fuck to do it!
Also the nappies they make him wear!
Also he wants an apple, and new teeth to eat it.
But in this place where he has recently landed,
which is where he has always been,
every day is day-after-day
so you cannot have everything,
the whole lot has to be later.

Listen hard now to how we all say goodbye
and maybe and wait-just-a-minute,
not hearing the world say back to us wow.
There's not much difference in it.
In this way you will get to hear
his very last sigh – the sound of a plane
powering down when it reaches the gate,
and all of us getting to our feet.

What I'm picking up when I'm out and about

Aristotle said that women shouldn't be allowed to drive cars. I think the jury's still
out on that one. He also said that we should look both ways before we cross the
road, and I think he was probably right about that.
+
Ursula Bethell and some of the other young people reckoned I should give it a shot
so I thought I might try writing a poem or two but well it's harder than it looks.
Sappho, she's about my age but she's all talk that one. Too much this, too much
that.
+
Aesop still going on about his fables. They get paid for this stuff.
+
I suppose those flying carpets really existed. They always look a bit uncomfortable
to me though I've never heard anyone complaining. Aladdin went for a ride on one
and I was a bit worried there for a while.
+
Of course Pluto's a planet. People live there. For god's sake let's just try to be
sensible why can't you.
+
You don't see pikelets around much these days. I've always liked a good pikelet.
+
Anyway Callimachus what kind of a name is that.

On Harold Bloom

Poetry, Psyche, God, Mortality

DAVID ROSENBERG

THE ABUNDANT IRONIES and critiques of literary fashion that enrich the unique writing style of Harold Bloom are glossed over by Zachary Leader in a recent *Times Literary Supplement* review of a suddenly posthumous book. The occasion is Bloom's 'last book' at age eighty-nine – though Bloom attested to a multitude of last books, starting at seventy-four, with his premonitions of health problems and mortality that were typical for his age. Of these last books, *The American Canon*, thoughtfully edited by David Mikics, is probably not the best. Yet it shouldn't take long before Bloom's historical competition rises into view; Leopardi, Samuel Johnson and the literary Freud among them.

In his review, Leader glosses over the substantive Bloomian texts which the title of the posthumous book encodes: *The American Religion* (1992) and *The Western Canon* (1995). Bloom himself, in this last 'last book', laments the lack of literary attention to the former, and the scarce consideration of the spiritual dimension to the latter. Both dimensions are first addressed in unison in *The Book of J* (1990), though the seeds were planted in Bloom's early studies of Milton, Blake and Yeats.

Leader writes that Bloom's 'appetite for words, coupled with a prodigious memory, lucrative book deals and his own eventual enthronement in the critical canon, made Bloom a central literary figure for the age'. This sounds generous at first, but look more closely: Bloom's critical acumen, built upon a complex aesthetic of psychological as well as historical perspective, is hardly recognized by an 'appetite for words'. His 'lucrative book deals' were the result of a startling transformation of writing style from elaborate litcrit to popular vernacular: it seemed to whisper plainly into the ear of the general reader without losing much of his intricate thought.

As for his 'enthronement'; goodness! Bloom brought to literary criticism a self-characterization redolent of Falstaff, not Henry. 'A rather plump and melancholy youth, I turned to him out of need, because I was lonely. Finding myself in him liberated me from a debilitating self-consciousness. He has never abandoned me for three-quarters of a century.' And, further from his *Falstaff: Give Me Life* (2017), probably his most poignant of last books: 'He exposes what is counterfeit in me and in all others.'

It's useful to unpack a bit more of Leader's review because the public image of Bloom as a 'central literary figure for the age' is too often based upon his legendary teaching persona at Yale rather than a close reading of his books. Not that he didn't yoke the professorial to the wish for a public spotlight, as in the political avocation (he called it 'prophecy') that could over-season his prose. 'We are living in a dark time' may be a common locution in academe these days, but this was Bloom in 2007, after it was clear the nation had survived the World Trade Center massacre, and less than a year before Obama's presidency. Bloom had remained in full BDS (Bush Derangement Syndrome) reaction, not content to refer to the president as 'an imbecile' in essays and reviews, even though the forty-third president may have received a passing grade as a student of his at Yale, where Bush not only graduated but went on to a graduate degree from Harvard. (On a personal note concerning this recent era of political apoplexy in the humanities: while we were at Berkeley the year Bush was elected, my wife Rhonda and I sometimes dined out with the late British philosopher Richard Wollheim, also on visiting faculty duty. Richard was beside himself the whole time, faux-interrogating us as to how an 'illiterate' like Bush could so intellectually incapacitate America. One answer, quaintly academic, invoked the influence of the literary history of American Puritanism, a required course of the Yale undergraduate curriculum, to explain erstwhile playboy Bush's long happy marriage to librarian Laura and how it cancelled the previous President Clinton's sexual exploits and cover-up.)

In the same *TLS*, Elaine Showalter laments that Bloom 'knew very little about feminist criticism'. Probably true, though he did read and reread women he loved; Emily Dickinson, H.D., and Zora Neale Hurston representing a diversity among them. Yet it is mind-boggling that Showalter fails to mention the great contribution to the history of female authorship, the Yahwist, designated J in biblical scholarship. *The Book of J* provided as much a provocation to misogyny and male literary dominance as any in the twentieth century, to say nothing of the feathers ruffled in religion departments. I can understand it sounds almost like a joke to assert that the great writer of the early Bible was a woman of ironic temperament who established the basis of biblical history at her post-Solomonic court, but that's merely a sign of how repressed the memory of human authorship remains. Far from simple speculation, our collaboration provides over three hundred pages of reality-testing evidence that J could be none other than a woman.

In her latest book, *The Lost Art of Scripture,* Karen Armstrong unfortunately bypasses biblical authorship altogether: 'Our English word "Scripture" implies a written text, but most Scriptures began as texts that were composed and transmitted orally.' This is an outdated claim; the word 'began' should begin in the biblical author's written sources. Lear, Hamlet, et.al. also began in old, possibly oral sources, but so what? The problem here is that Armstrong is content to imply that Hebraic literate poets and prose artists, along with their artistic culture and education – drawing upon more than a millennium of written (in cuneiform, Egyptian demotic, etc.) classics –

need not be considered. In contrast to Armstrong's literary incuriosity, another new book, Michael Schmidt's *Gilgamesh,* brings the Akkadian written sources clearly into view, including layers of authorship dating back many centuries to the Sumerian Odes in cuneiform tablets – texts that were probably accessible to early Hebraic authors as well.

We need to pause here with *The Book of J* because it represents the crucial pivot at which Bloom's academic writing morphed into the popular vernacular. While Leader asserts 'Bloom's critical fame rested largely on his book *The Anxiety of Influence* (1973)', news of Bloom's stature did not reach the general reader until *The Book of J*'s ironic renderings of foundational patriarchs and matriarchs, Abraham and Sarah, Isaac and Rebecca, Jacob and Rachel. That surprising bestseller presented a way to understand poetry and poetic prose outside the contemporary academic norms. As well, in this first and last published collaboration of Bloom's, we took Biblical source criticism two human footsteps further by pressing on through the text to characterize the fleshly writers behind it, culminating in the figure of J as a royal court-educated woman. It was fairly in tune with Bloom's characterizations of major poets, from Chaucer to Ashbery, as personalities with larger cultural concerns, such as Ashbery's parallel life as an art critic.

Had Armstrong absorbed Bloom's insights on authorship, she might have resisted her prejudicial claim that the Hebrew Bible repeatedly has God ordering genocides. This was far more likely a literary trope, elaborated from sources that sought to allegorize a monotheistic God's determination to complete a 'genocide' of his *own* rivals; namely the panoply of pagan gods and idols. We needn't go so far, however, as to 'prize the astonishing mystery of creative genius', as Adam Begley long ago asserted in the *New York Times* was Bloom's master plan. In literary terms today, it is not a 'mystery' but a poetics of process; a modernist engine Bloom unfortunately seemed to reject, even in Stevens and Ashbery. The term collage eludes him, especially in relation to modern masters for whom dissipation and loss of control are integrated into the work. He would not likely consider how a lyric poem built upon collage and improvisation is nonetheless held together by the non-mysterious gravitational force of meditative focus, as in Sylvia Plath, a poet Bloom avoided, as he did the New York School poets Ted Berrigan and David Shapiro.

I've written about my three-year collaboration with Bloom while he was still alive, in *A Life in a Poem,* yet some excerpts in this posthumous context are newly applicable to an appreciation of his limits as well as his pre-eminence:

It was the strangest thing about Harold, especially as I reflect on it now, that he was almost incapable of punning, especially in informal conversation. He might quote one, from Shakespeare, for instance, but for himself he seemed always to shy away, as if a pun were a kind of poem and that it would imperil his credentials as a critic to be revealed as a poet – or anything less than a major poet. Too bad he couldn't have become a critic in Yiddish, as if there'd been no Holocaust and the great Jewish language of his and my youth had continued to exfoliate. There his punning would have bloomed, beyond the highly literary sort disguised as irony. He might

have merited a Nobel, like Isaac Bashevis Singer, had he become the great Jewish critic.

So Harold was no deconstructionist, and that viewpoint's wealth of puns, its insistence on punning, as in the poetry of David Shapiro, scared him. He wouldn't admit to being upset in this way, but rather dismissed Shapiro as not up to the standard of his mentor, Ashbery. To call David a deconstructionist in poetry might be an understatement; his every line recomposed the previous, fearless to employ any pun at any moment. Because he was a close friend of mine, I tried whenever possible to strengthen his case with Harold, insinuating how he was a beloved presence in the 'Second Generation' of New York School poets. I was insensitive, however, to how the mere existence of that school – so at home with the pun and with the French modernists who had deeply domesticated it – was in itself the bane of Harold's role as critic of the latest in contemporary poetry. As I've said before, I could not get him to read the New York School masters; O'Hara, Schuyler, and especially Kenneth Koch, whose ingenious punning disturbed him and whose Ivy League position at Columbia enervated him (until, worn down at last, he wrote sympathetically of Koch in the late '90s). Although Ashbery was also of this school, Harold separated him out as a poet akin to himself, full of strange ironies more grandiose than the lowly pun. Before I'd fully realized this I did Shapiro no little harm in Bloom's eyes by pointing out Koch as his true mentor. However, I was alert enough not to refer to my own coming to maturity among second generation New York School poets, nor to my having been a student of Koch's before that.

Keeping this thought to myself, I imagined Marcel Duchamp as a major twentieth-century counterpart to Bloom, the former exerting a greater influence over American artists than Bloom among poets. Yet Bloom was just as concerned to challenge the definition of poetry as Duchamp was of art. 'I am an experiential and personalizing literary critic', wrote Bloom, 'which certainly rouses up enmity, but I go on believing poems matter only if we matter'. This was less in tune with prevailing ambition among MFA and PhD poets than with Virginia Woolf's 'insistence that a work cannot be understood without knowledge of the circumstances of its creation'. Cultural context, in other words. Although Bloom lacked sufficient awareness of other contemporary arts, including art, film, music, and dance ('confined to this hick town of New Haven', as he once confided), he brought considerable modern context to poetry in the form of his psychological translation of Freud into an account of poetic ambition, as well his personal experience of facing the Holocaust and how lack of it underwrites a contemporary resistance to history. Such contextual thought also led to his wider interest in religion and ancient culture, specifically to *The Book of J* and J's literary situation in ancient Jerusalem (with Bloom's concerns in mind, I went on to point out her cultural surround, from Hebraic sculptors to composers, in later books).

In *The American Religion,* Bloom compares 'self-creation', as elsewhere manifested in the close reading of Walt Whitman, to mythological creation: 'each of us is subject and object of the one quest, which must be for the original self, a spark or breath in us that we are convinced goes back to before the Creation.' If Bloom was constantly thinking of self-creation, Duchamp was thinking of its context, physical existence, a surround that requires our artistic awareness of being a created artifact of ourselves. Duchamp was on a mission to 'break into' that artifact, whether a painting (the third dimension of 'Nude Descending a Staircase') or a theory of breathing. Starting with 'Fountain' in 1917, a urinal turned into a sculpture, Duchamp had defined art as a choosing, but later, in a 1965 interview with Pierre Cabanne, he says 'My art would be that of living; each second, each breath is a work which is inscribed nowhere, which is neither visual nor cerebral'. Existence, in other words, as rich context.

Bloom, on the other hand, was usually thinking of 'breaking out' of existence into the cosmic, whether the supernatural mythos of Blake in London, or in the manner of J in Jerusalem, recording the speech of the monotheistic God. Implicit, of course, was the understanding that the supernatural cosmos is theory, and just as intellectually pregnant as science theory. It needn't be proved psychologically any more than the interior of a black hole requires physical proof. Beyond Northrup Frye, a precursor, Bloom raised the act of writing literary criticism to the level of cosmic drama – no less than Duchamp had shifted the perspective of an artwork back onto its existential viewer. One might argue the same for Picasso and others, except that Duchamp's oeuvre points beyond the artistic process of a human creator plumbing consciousness, and toward the species-consciousness of that creator as a Homo sapiens within an evolutionary process.

A word more on process, since it relates to the contemporary poetry which Bloom was averse to access, yet illustrates his personal exodus over the years from modernism. It's not that he was constitutionally constricted but that he'd found a way within the academic world to express what I can only call a spiritual process – one in blind parallel to the experimental process of American poetry (as well as remaining innocent of a British Bunting). Religious books for Bloom could be not simply poetic but poetry itself; cosmic poetry. It was hardly a matter of being influenced by Milton and Blake. What modern literary critic could you possibly find who would produce a six hundred paged anthology of *American Religious Poems* (2006)? Bloom is not joking; he's deadly serious about collecting his usual suspects, including hundreds of pages of living and mostly academic poets demonstrating a prayer-like stance toward a 'religion' that is in fact devoutly anti-transcendent. Nevertheless, the poems of Bloom's contemporary poets read as if plotted – nothing processual, abstract, or post-Avant – hence not a whiff in them of, God forbid, Jesus or God, or even a tenuous relation to Geoffrey Hill.

Instead, Bloom incarnates them as followers of the Whitmanian religion of self-creation. Black Mountain, however, or the New York School, doesn't exist, with the exception of Ashbery misinterpreted as metaphysical. The Objectivists are reduced to a little poem observing wild deer by Oppen, and one by Reznikoff entitled 'Spinoza' – nothing of his volumes of Biblical intertexts. As for the post-Avant and experimental, not even a Jackson Mac Low 'Light Poem' (e.g. number thirty-two mourning Paul Blackburn) or the North American epic *The Martyrology* of bpNichol, let alone Robin Blaser's *The Holy Forest*. No whiff of the transcendental air in a Lorine Niedecker, and no Ted Berrigan, so many of whose

non-collagist poems, rather than somewhat engaging prayerfulness, resonate as transcendent adorations of daily life. And then there is the egregious ignoring of Gertrude Stein's astonishing and existentially religious *The Making of Americans* (only the photographic reading ability of Harold Bloom might have committed its 926 pages to memory).

And yet, none of the present, let alone the missing, could have been collared by anyone but Bloom in service to the ongoing vitality of poetry: namely, his gorgeous elaboration of Whitman and Dickinson as the seeders and binders of an American Canon. That he refused to consider improvisation is probably why he could never write a poem of his own. But also why he took the inspired improvisations of Walt and Emily to be forms of thought more significant than music – and thus able to arrive at the proper determination anyway that their projection of themselves in terms of self-created character was as if open-ended, a boundless energy no poet who followed could, or can, as yet, rival.

Bloom's introduction to *American Religious Poems* is, in particular, an apotheosis of Whitman as our American Shakespeare, Dante, Christ, Yahweh, Adam, Blake, Hopkins – all these and more he adumbrates. Bloom also focuses upon how 'Whitman owed far more to the English Bible than to any particular poet', especially J's Yahweh: his 'I am' and his 'Get thee out' to Abraham (ironically echoing the directive to Adam and Eve, to leave the Garden, and later to the Exodus). But – where to? To an as yet unknown destination, re-echoed in Whitman and his influence on American poets from Hart Crane to Frank O'Hara's visionary 'Second Avenue'. For Walt Whitman, the journey had blossomed inward, so that 'the shores of America matter most to Whitman as points of departure for the outward voyage. [But again, to where?] There is only the grand fourfold: night, death, the mother, and the sea. All of these constitute the unknown nature of which Walt's soul is composed'.

In fact, Bloom here strives to create a matching Bloomian selfhood as *reader*, one who is breaking out on a voyaging duet with his time-bound aging self. Yet I fear Harold may have missed the pun on his name in his concluding paragraph: 'Finally, Whitman is the American difference, the herald to the future.' There is no Duchampian breaking in, something to be accomplished by turning consciousness inside out, escaping beyond human history to an evolutionary origin. Duchamp's duet entails an unknown species, one that is abstracted in poetry as improvisation. Meanwhile, our cultural history is repressed, an unconsciously purposeful forgetting, a la Freud. To what end, what progress? A duet with creation is the answer, as it collects one's art, one's lifetime of objects, in miniature, placing them in a suitcase as Duchamp did, suggesting an embarkation as a reborn child. Where to? One would love to hear that question debated between Duchamp and Bloom, less with theory than with a wagon full of art and poetry books.

Bloom's suitcases, however, had so much more textual history in them that an endless stream of porters would be required. And yet, it's instructive to suggest how he might have looked by traveling with simply a carry-on, like Duchamp's little suitcase. Still, if we imagine a Duchamp retrospective in another century it is massive;

it will have to resemble the current one of Blake at Tate Britain, organized in a contextual framework of Blake's historical situation. For the experimental modern poets who Bloom generally avoided, Ashbery may serve as stand-in. 'His mode can vary from the apparently opaque, so disjunctive as to seem beyond interpretation, to a kind of limpid clairvoyance.' However, the 'disjunctive' in Ashbery is often hilarious rather than opaque, its collaging of seemingly overheard snippets a contemporary form of punditry (or of an unattended mind). Yet it can also produce a deep poignance in its failure to alleviate the anxiety of mortality, which is suggested by the sources of either the overheard or the underlying art of, for instance, fragmented body parts, the alphabet or paintings by Holbein (e.g. 'An Allegory of the Old and New Testaments, 1533-35') in the contemporary art of Jasper Johns.

Even the way language is out of tune with thought may produce both anxiety and comedy in younger counterparts of Ashbery; e.g. Mark Ford and Susan Wheeler, whom Bloom did find a way to appreciate. Nevertheless, he would be apt to elide the comedy as he did most surprisingly when he judged Rimbaud to be a younger counterpart to Blake: 'Rimbaud was a great innovator within French Poetry, but he would have seemed less so had he written in the language of Blake and Wordsworth, Browning and Whitman. *A Season in Hell* comes more than eighty years after *The Marriage of Heaven and Hell*.' It's also likely that were Bloom's double to return to us in fifty years, his expansive perspective might enfold as well the contemporaries he side-stepped.

In their introduction to the current Blake show's catalogue, Myrone and Concannon say 'we think it matters where and when these artworks were created'. Yet much is missing when Blake's theory of consciousness goes unmentioned. I use 'theory' to update 'myth', emphasizing that Blake included the bottomless unconscious mind – in such forms as Satan and angels – as vital mirror to the human situation. Forgetting the pull of the unconscious, we put too much stress today on society, on social relations public and private, to interpret such complex behaviour as the making of art. Blake would have made an avid reader of Freud's *Leonardo da Vinci: A Psychosexual Study of an Infantile Reminiscence*. Blake's own art is portrayed by Bloom as a significant instance of unconscious creative struggle with Milton, comparable to a modern American poet's struggle with Whitman. In this manner, we might also surmise that Blake's Emily Dickinson, were she his precursor, would actually be not her, of course, but Michelangelo.

Speaking for the moment of duets, and as much as he digs deeper than anyone could expect into Stevens and Frost, Bloom retained a blind spot regarding modernism up until his end. He recognizes it, of course, and justifies his aversion by pointing to modernism's displeasure with history, its delight in fragmentation and flouting of tradition. Although it would seem Bloom enjoyed similar traits, starting with his pushing of Blake to the forefront (it's worth remembering that most everyone from Pound and Eliot to Stevens and Auden were ambivalent about Blake), what he found in him was of a piece with Shakespeare; namely a confrontation with not only the full scope of human history (one could cite Pound's sweep from ancient Egyptian, Greek, and Chinese poetry, on

through the Troubadours and Dante, to Yeats and an ephebe in Olson) but the dimensions of the psyche. For Bloom, a civilizational sweep such as Pound's also swept under the rug the psychological price of rebellion against the humanistic history based in the Bible. 'My "favourite" remark of his, humanly and critically', said Bloom of Pound, 'comes from his letters: "All the Jew part of the Bible is black evil."' But it's not a critical duet, such as one between Bloom and New Testament-favouring Eliot, that he was after. Starting with his book *Poetry and Repression* (1976) and still manifest in his last book, it was the poetic duets of the biblically-grounded Whitman or Dickinson with every American poet onward that Bloom spun out in existentially religious terms.

So, *pace* Blake, it was not modernist supersession itself that worried Bloom but its grandiosities and self-congratulation, its lack of self-criticism. Ironically enough, however, Bloom overlooked the grandiosity in himself when he dismissed modern experimental duets. It seems quite probable there could be no Lorine without Emily, no William Carlos Williams without Walt, nor especially the experimental duets of modern poets with language itself, of musicians with composition, or of painters with viewers, much of it incomprehensibly dissonant to Bloom's ear. He would attempt to compensate with gnostic theories of unrepressed vitality, and although he could filter Ashbery and Anne Carson through Stevens, the latter's self-aware engagement with the psyche remained the crucial element for Bloom. Still, he had found his own way to read living poets in psychological terms, the 'poetic misprisions' (clinamen, tessera, kenosis, askesis, apophrades, daemonization – swerving, completing, emptying, truncating, returning to/opening up, displacing) that made up the literary family drama.

A contemporary of Bloom's, the Jewish avant saxophonist, Lee Konitz, still breathing in Brooklyn, built an oeuvre riffing on standards, just as Harold would point out Walt on Bible, Emily on Shakespeare's sonnets. Yet Bloom was circumscribed from the most anxious or avant-garde of his living culture, for him a seemingly adversarial post-academe. What could he do with it, since he had no creative practice of his own? Or rather, he strove to make his critical writing a proto-Kabbalist art of riffing on a canon that could be seen from above and included everything, even the Lee Konitz album *Duets* of which he was innocent. It was a striving constrained, however, by limited access to the quotidian that was a breakthrough resource for his younger artistic contemporaries. In place of the historical, poets Lewis Warsh and Bernadette Mayer, in their just-published (small portions appeared in the 1970's) *Piece of Cake* ('arguably the first significant male-female collaboration in twentieth century American poetry') riff on an immediate history of daily life. Unlike earlier modernists such as Picabia collaging newsprint and Reznikoff accessing documents, they move in and occupy a dailiness that Proust ironized by retrieving memories (or that was called 'the banality of everyday life' in the Danish painter Hammershoi). As children of the sixties, they seemed to break down the border between life and art, yet Mayer and Warsh's domesticated stream of consciousness can be gloriously deadpan (another term missing from Bloom's vocabulary) just as the late British poet Andrew Crozier, a literary countercultural parallel, could inhabit an intellectual deadpan that was provocatively non-dry.

Bloom was unlikely to hear those riffs and thus would not fully appreciate the improvisation in Ashbery, and especially not in Berrigan, whose 'Ted' is in duet with himself. What had already been assimilated in the 1930's as absurdist literature now steps beyond the absurdity of daily life and the human condition, and into a hyper-reality that casts the poem itself as absurd – though not forgetting that it is the tenderest form of communication.

> What emerges as authentic from that breakdown (and it can resemble a useful literary nervous breakdown) is the poet at his writing table, anchored at the scene of writing, more human than ever. He writes in 'Wishes':

> Wish I were walking around in Chelsea (NY) & it was 5:15 a.m., the sun coming up, alone, you asleep at home...

> At home during the scene of writing the poem, Berrigan is not 'walking around', except in his mind. *That* Berrigan, the one walking the streets – who really embodies such flaneur behaviour elsewhere in this and other poems – remains marginal compared to the writer at his desk (who really is at the page's margin, creature-wise, and is the truer subject of the poem). So what enriches this art is that it never settles for the poetic but rather assumes a poker face of playing for higher stakes.

At the time I did not know how to elaborate the context for Bloom to read such contemporary work. Collage and the quotidian, while basic to modernism, could become in the postmodern canon the very breath itself, *pace* Duchamp, from Olson to Berrigan. In a British analogy to the deadpan inferred from the American Objectivists or the New York School, and similarly attuned to painting, contemporary London poet Anthony Rudolf, an important tragicomic post-Objectivist in disguise as a European cosmopolitan, collapses the distance between art and daily life, text and 'unwritten' breathing, in his self-duet:

> ....it's poems
> written that are lost for ever,
> unwritten ones always remain
> to be found. Like Morandi
> painting variations on
> the same theme, it has taken me
> twenty years to get the picture.

Here in 'Found Poem', conventional expectations of the poem are emptied out, leaving as residue the poet himself. Probably Bloom wouldn't recognize that, just as it wasn't the figure of Blake behind his poem that revealed itself to Bloom. More certainly, it was Blake's mind, conscious and unconscious, his epic determination to see contemporary English culture in Biblical dimensions. And that was how J did it in Genesis, allowing Bloom to elaborate on how her mythic characters were purposefully modelled on her near-contemporaries, such as Jacob on King David, or Rachel on David's daughter, Tamar.

Would Bloom be excited by the current Blake show and its accompanying catalogue? Naturally he'd miss more of the actual poems, the illuminated book pages, but if you could imagine a similar exhibition for J's lost manuscripts of which he'd approve, it would also include chapters on how, nearly three thousand years ago, she was educated, apprenticed, her family life, how she earned a living, where she lived and in what circumstances, the ancient equivalent of artistic guilds, etc. Most crucial for Bloom would be her precursors among writers and scholars, and not only in Hebrew but in the ancient transnational classics. If any one of them had writers as original as J, it would have been evident in their own linguistic traditions, as we've begun to see in the contextual study of the Akkadian Gilgamesh epic.

What Bloom means by J's 'originality' is that, like Blake, she (or if we remain stubborn, 'the text') refocused what came before with such forceful irony that it transcends the comic and infuses its sources with the principle of reality-testing. Bloom's most significant education here came via Freud – though he'd later suggest the Kabbalah as a form of imaginative analysis of both experience and, in the voluminous instance of the *Zohar*, Biblical and Talmudic text. In between Freud and the Kabbalah (and the classroom textual analysis that was translated into popular commercial ventures, notably with Shakespeare) came the seminal *The Book of J*. Here is a scene from how it first took shape:

> I recall a time when you lectured a conference of New York psychoanalysts on the many impersonations Freud suggested for the ego – much to their puzzlement – but now, among your several iterations of Hamlet, you posit that his 'I's are infinite, by which you mean unknowable, and that human consciousness is as well, in line with the contemporary fashion in high-end poetry. Do you remember how we came to my literary agent at the time, Lynn Nesbit, with the proposal for our collaboration on *The Book of J*? You were quaking with guilt, wondering if you'd be able to postpone the contract you were already under with Viking for a life of Freud. 'Let's just cancel it', she said. Afterward, you were so relieved to not have to write that book that you kissed me. It was some time later you told me you had similarly 'cancelled' your psychoanalyst, who dared admonish you (so it seemed to you) to leave out lengthy literary quotations from your free-association during sessions.

Central to *The Book of J* was the character of the monotheistic God, originally named Yahweh, or Jehovah in English mis-transliteration. For myself, in answer to the existence of God question, I affirmed belief while I read, doubt when outside the text. Bloom argued further, for belief when reciting – as he could anywhere and at anytime, possessed by a prodigious memory. Thus Bloom transmuted the God question into the human question, namely self-creation, which took him from Freud to Shakespeare and Whitman as prime instances of originality and its influences on English-language poetry.

There could be no self-creation, however, without the original character of Yahweh. In his intro to *American Religious Poems*, Bloom writes: 'Yahweh, in my speculative judgment, can be said to have (first) come into existence by saying *I Am*... Whitman palpably opposes *I Am* to *It Was*... [Like most North American poets who followed] Walt proclaims his presence but cultivates absence: he is sly, evasive, self-contradictory.'

Those last descriptors apply to J's Yahweh in Genesis

and Exodus, where the cosmic theatre of the unknowable heavens requires a covenant between unknowable Creator and his Hebrew-writing human creations. Bloom further boiled down the Hebraic cosmic theatre into an existential human theatre to accommodate English-language poetry (Wordsworth, a poet he left largely to his Yale colleague Geoffrey Hartman, is Bloom's British equivalent to Whitman). Yet what's left behind in the Bible is a more capacious sense of the unknowable – or, as Freud represented it, the unconscious. As I wrote about this to Harold within *A Life in a Poem*:

> ...consciousness has become the be-all and end-all of contemporary literary knowledge, even though the father of it all, Freud, was sceptical of marginalizing the unconscious. Today, consciousness has appropriated the unconscious within itself, along with a totalizing scepticism; consciousness is so enshrined, so honourable in theory of mind or art, that only the counter-scepticism of a neuroscientist – whose unconscious is out-of-sight, out-of-mind – worries it, albeit slightly. Clearly you have struggled to outflank any doubt about the supremacy of consciousness by creating a character of yourself, dramatized by your self-possessed self-consciousness, and you brilliantly displayed it in your lecture tonight when you faux-apologized for the ambiguity in a sentence you'd just delivered from your lecture's manuscript: 'I've looked at it many times, to see if I could clarify it further, but I've failed. So let me repeat it.' If it had been a joke, the repetition would have killed it, but in this case (it really *was* a joke in disguise), by repeating it, it came to sound strangely indelible, as if it belonged in the Bible's *Book of Proverbs*.

As became increasingly clear in his last books, Bloom's own self-creation rivalled the literary characters he invoked, from Hamlet to 'Walt', though none so ineffable as J's literary characterization of Yahweh. What had been an encounter with the supernatural devolved into the human psyche. Something crucial, however, had been lost in Bloom's late psychology, something Blake would have noted: Judeo-Christian religion's evocation of the unconscious – in biblical terms of the supernatural – had dug an even deeper literary well into the Homo sapiens psyche.

Finally, we might acknowledge as Bloom's signal accomplishment that he raised literary criticism, as I've said, to the level of cosmic drama. His representation of the psyche as a contest between the self-created and its adversary, mortality, allows us to read Shakespeare and the Bible on an even playing field.

The newspaper obits noted that Bloom at eighty-nine, quite ill, had willed himself to teach his last class just three days before his death. It turns out that he actually missed just one gig, on the day before his dying, a lecture he was scheduled to deliver from home via Skype to a conference of San Francisco psychoanalysts. No doubt he would still have been testing his agon with Freud. And in so doing, Bloom would have raised both, Freud and himself, to the level of self-created literary characters, hence capable of surviving death, just as Oedipus and Hamlet are still with us. Better yet, even as resolved into a literary character, there is no question Yahweh remains beyond death, turning 'death of God' thoughts into linguistic irony on a par with 'I am that I am'. We might say with Bloom that God was deadpan in this revelation to Moses. Although Bloom's term for deadpan was 'strange', it likewise suggested that Yahweh was as immortally unknowable as the later Hebraic elaboration of him as unnameable. In the sense of strangeness Bloom cultivated, we might call the literary character he made of himself a transcendent reader, post-mortal. Thus he is only half-joking when he writes, 'since I am two decades older than [Anne] Carson, one of my likely regrets when I depart is that I will not have absorbed her lifetime's work'.

Spolia

To my Father

MARIA STEPANOVA

Translated by Sasha Dugdale

THE TRANSLATOR WRITES: *Spolia* is the Latin word for 'spoils', as in 'the spoils of war'. It was introduced to the field of art history at the turn of the sixteenth century to describe the ancient marble ornaments embedded in medieval settings. The term enfolds the principle and theme of Maria Stepanova's long poem: that language and culture are translated and transported as fragments and re-used in new settings and to new ends. 'Spolia' was written in the summer of 2014, at a time when Russia had occupied the Crimea and hostilities between Russia and Ukraine were fierce. The poem draws the subjectivity of a woman, a poet, a country and a history into one rich and complex skein. The original poem uses quotes from non-Russian poets (such as Walt Whitman) and Russian poets (such as Mikhail Kuzmin). In the translation I have extended that principle and added in fragments of other English-language poets, because the vitality and wit and sadness of the poem seemed to demand this.

totted up
what was said
amounted to

she simply isn't able to speak for herself
and so she always uses rhyme in her poems

ersatz and out of date poetic forms

her material
offers no resistance
its kiss is loveless, it lies motionless

she's the sort you'd lift onto a chair
read us the poem about wandering lonely

she's the sort who once made a good Soviet translator

careful unadventurous

where is her *I* place it in the dish
why on earth does she speak in voices

(voices 'she has adopted', in quote marks:
obvs anyone-without-an-I cannot adopt anything
for anyone-without-an-I will wander, begging alms
pretending to be a corner, a jar of mayonnaise, a cat
although no one believes him quite)

I'm a bagel I'm a bagel says the speaker-without-an-I
some people are stuffed with soft cheese but oh no not me
some people are engorged with character and culture
potato scones, hot stones,
I've got the biggest hole empty yawning
I'm the earth I send my cosmonauts floating

the mouths of my eaters, the teeth of my tenants,
converging from the east and the south,
they take a last chew   swallow

when a quick nought has licked up the last crumb
fire's sharp tongue will scour the granaries –

I won't even remain as air, shifting
refracting sound
fading with the light on the river's ripple
sucking the milk and vodka from still-moist lips

anyone-without-an-I
is permitted a non-i-ppearance
wants libert-i

Tramcar, tramcar, squat and wide!
Pushkin pops his clogs inside!
Dingle-dangle Pushkin-Schmushkin
Dying cloudberries in the bushkin
Demigod   theomorph
Dig the burning peaty turf

Innokenty Annensky
Stuck between *here*sky and *there*sky

Is feeling miserably empty
At the station in Tsarskoselsky

All the hungry passengers
Waiting in the railway shack
Say Look! A Bone is stuck in your Throat!
But the bone is red-lipped gabriak.

No I won't be your good boy,
The teenage poet blurts –
Voloshin can have his way with them
Stick his fingers up their skirts,
Crimean wine, bearded philanderer...
Now Blok appears – is gone again
Under the sun of Alexander
Polyakov picks up the reins.

Ancient Scythian stone women
Glow as they crumble
Instagram posts for Soviet airmen,
Seizing wheatears as they scramble
Now fire the search engine!
Fix eyepiece on the earth's sphere!
Glazova and Barskova
are coming over loud and clear.

There was an old woman who lived in a shoe
All the poets were full of woe
And nobody knew what to do.

Dying, like clearing out a room
without making a fuss
resurrection, if and when

---

visible delicate
invisible inviolate
nearest dearest
souring, steeping
delayed *en route*
root of the
wormwood
clamped
in the teeth
wordeed
wordtree
word wood
beasting
the unbested
suspended, resisted

put by in secrets

halfcracked   halfvolk

---

let her come out herself and say something
(and we'll listen to you)
she won't come out
it won't come right

speaks from the heart
(tchaikovsky! let me die but first)
but she says it like she doesn't mean it
it even seems like her words
might have come from someone else
always over-stylising
like she's dressing a corpse

where's her inimitable intonation
the breath catching in her throat
that individual stamp
recognisable from a single note
(the work of an engineer and not of a poet)

(not lyrics, mechanics –
signs not of a lady but of a mechanic)

and these *projects* all the time
as if the cold sweat of inspiration
on her forehead never made her hair stand on

enough, I said, I'm prigov
you prigs can fuck off

---

when blossoms tum-ti-tum
for the last time the blossom
in the dooryard bloomed
the lilac in the dooryard bloomed

and stars that shoot along the sky
not yet will measureless fields be green
and dancing by the light of the moon
the light of the moon

and after April when May follows
banquet halls up yards and bunting-dressed
and breasts stuck white with wreath and spray
marked off the girls unreally from the rest
who lined the sidings grimly gay

(she loves embedding quotes because
she can't be without love)

washed by the rivers blest by the suns of home

my land, I love your vast expanses!
your steppe & coachmen, costumed dances!
your peddlars of mystic trances!

and murdered Tsar Nicholas
oh, and Kitezh's watery kingdom
and how above our golden freedom
rises gloom dusk cumulus

how early that star drooped in the chilled Western air
I'll remember May the First and the scent of your hair
when for the last time
when we saw

last one to the gate is a rotten egg
and they run and run

----

and so I decided
I was told

curly feathers of metro marble
milk white enamel girls
in gilded kazakh skull caps
and children with gently determined faces
you, blue-eyed aeronauts and machine gunners
saboteurs, cavalrymen and tank drivers
fringe-finned guardsmen, officers
platforms of shaggy crouching partisans
and especially the border guard's alsatian

plum blossom in a golden bowl
early morning crimea
ballerina winding herself widdershins
apollo in singlet and hockey shorts
alabaster profile on wedgwood medallion
clearly sketched in a golden oval
aeroplane wreathing omens in the clouds
hercules, given to omphale

you must have forgotten

in the passageway leading to the circle line

Do you remember, Maria
our twilit corridor
nineteen-forties Russia
a settlement, post war
dances to the radiogram
twostep at arm's length
freight trains loaded
with gold and frankincense
those hard done hard won
those barely alive
down on your bare knees
a head against your thigh
tea twinkles in the strainer
steams in the room
bulbous iron knobs
where a cheap dress is thrown
remember how she stood
weeping on the porch
when they hunted him down
caught him in the church
smiling, he was led
looked back as if to say
then a round in the head
and a truck sped away
at the crack of fire
you turned and left
and cranked up your life
and lived it cleft.

---

my brother said you're a fascist
you sing up, and I'll sing loud
we'll be back when the trees are in leaf
but I'll stand my ground

when the leaves are in fist
and the deer dances past the oak
the antifascist flips to fascist
and the wood goes for broke

words are attached to things
with old twine
and people lay down with their tubers
in the ground for all time

but them, they cross yards
with lists and chalk
and lick the paint off window sills
with tongues that fork

fascist fattish fetish
flatfish, flippery, facetious
but the air knows we're not of them,
none of you or us.

untie the words
let them lie desperate, without glory
and the wood will call back its men
non omnis moriar.

---

across the vast rippling sound
under the evening star
from the furthest shore
floated a wooden box

you couldn't hear any captain aboard
you couldn't see any sailors
all you could see a faint flickering light

(it floated closer to our home)

all you could hear   a faint scratching
as if something was awake in the case but crumbling
shifting handful by handful

all you could hear   the dripping and crackling
     of wax
and water psalm by psalm
read then washed away
then read and washed away

forgive me forgive me my friend
let me perish
it isn't about that

don't run along the shore after me
along a path that doesn't exist
legs collapsing under you
don't look for my wooden box
bobbing in the shallows
caught in the reeds

and most of all: don't take off the lid
turn your back on the old world
don't take off my lid

don't go back to mother
don't wander the villages speaking
from lips chalky white petrified
dear comrades brothers and sisters we happy few

---

depart from me for I am a sinful man
said the eagle to the headwind

depart from me for I am an infirm man
said the red clay to the hands

depart from me
I am not man at all
I am a recording device

trrrrrr chirr churr
bring a jug bring a jug

---

and snow fell, and it was kind of:

the azure light disappeared like a cataract

---

under the spindle of a low sky
a dust trail on the near shore
two cars, a Yawa motorbike
a woman in a scarf, her face hidden

the young are beautiful, the old are more so

a shop without a signboard
loaves of bread on the shelf
in rows like soldiers on parade
still warm to the touch

each loaf reluctantly cooling

by the factory gates
a briar rose in raspberry cuffs
points in its madness
to where the sickening smell comes from

where did you get to, mr speaker
from the regional office

how long, my dear
have we been travelling
over this bridge in our little car
will we ever leave this place

---

the high towers are lit up red
and on them tall flags are talking
in the skies the stars assemble in rows
and jet planes, rising

tanks on parade with heavy paunches
armoured chariots
dolphin-heroes
swallow-martyrs
lions picked for their stature, their roar
people people and people

above them floats apple blossom
scented buds of white acacia
crinkle-edged paper poppies
heads
on poles

---

apparition of these faces in the metro
lamps on a wet black wire

Instead of scribbles in soft pencil lead:
Spinnrade   the brook   the mill weir,
You find the homunculus stone dead
His foetal hands pressed to his ears,
And guards to the left and the right of the door
And *the party spirit in proletarian literature*
You'll stand in the entrance hall to read your verse
The stitches drawn so tight you'll forget all the words.

Plush Soviet rose
Drilling the briar shoot
But the shoot sows
Itself silently, hides deep among the roots
You beat to death those without babble
And honour those without grace
But if you look with a gaze that is level
The spines have grown on your face.

See how Pushkin's cobbler
Measures the foot with a sole
The litigant follows his example
And the author is tied to a pole.
But it's Pushkin's miller!
The auditorium is slowly filling
A re-educated pine tall as a pillar
Stretches   confesses it was once a willow

....

<insert hole in bagel here>

---

and so I decided
it was told to me that I should think back

so I thought back
and remembered

and it upset me
so I went and died

I died
and nothing came of it
apart from books
which came at some point
after fifty years

and former men
lost the form they once had

---

tell her to come out and say something
(*coo-ey*! calls war)
and the dog-heart growls and shrinks
and the son is born on the barracks floor

two friends lived like *ya* and *you*
and if one of them said yes
the underground water rose in the darkness
I'll sing of that soon

no says the other
no and that is an end
there are no children in the army
which is made up of many men

but there was nothing to say to your friends
when *I* sprang forth
between tree bole and gun bore
the cradle was caught

---

before the great war the apples were so fine
you might have heard that once at market – but who's
    left alive

---

click
trigger (shutter) cocked
chink   viewfinder   sight

the photographer takes the picture
(things are taken from their places)

trans-ferr-al
and trans-ition trans-lates the space anew
(where corpses lie alongside the quick)
trans-humans transhumance
ex-isled con-sumers
jesters creatives
students
peasants
(great-grandfather Grigory with his two hands
factory machine will chew off the right hand, but later,
great-grandfather whose face I never saw)
gawpers and gazers, proceeding arm-in-arm
and jews unassigned scattered
(we-jews)

o what bewildering confusion
from wild profusion

click

springtime, green garden, maytime

brooch at her throat, hair gathered in a bun
my grandmother (only a little older than me)
feeding a squirrel in a park on the outskirts of moscow

lonely soldier drinking mineral with syrup

school uniform, fitting room, apron-winged, unhemmed

festive streets, the houses and pavements illuminated in
    tiny lights

five-year-old mother flicks her silken ribbon
looks

click
click

wide-hipped rowing boats drawn up on the shore
their hulls bright in the sun
gondola swings flying over the abyss

a gypsy camp by the roadside, surly children in
    headscarves

home for former revolutionaries, two old ladies on a
    bench
(one is mine)

crimea, nineteen thirty seven, cascades of bathing
    beauties

(oh how you)

croquet on the dacha lawn, Moscow region

twenty years later in forty three
siberia, in evacuation
a headless cockerel and it swooped dead through the
    yard

head lying in the grass

and all the radio stations of the soviet union are
    speaking

accountant overwhelmed by numbers

nurse   (made it to berlin)

seventeen-year-old nanny

shoeshiner from the next stairwell

geologist recently released from his second sentence

gynaecologist

lecturer at the institute of architecture

vasya (who?) from solyanka street

woman from local health inspectorate

twenty-year-old lyodik killed in action

his father, a volunteer, bombed troop train

his mother who lived right up until death

a little girl who will remember all this

relatives from saratov and leningrad
inhabitants of khabarovsk and gorky
and those I have forgotten

and pushkin pushkin of course

everyone round a laden table
ninth of may victory celebration
windows thrown back radio on

victoria herself sitting at the table
singing the blue scarf song singing schubert
as if there were no death

---

so what bounds Russia, said the crippled man
you know very well what bounds it, said the crippled
    man
and every span of her earth
and every step in her dust
is a step towards border control
across no man's land
and the sky drawn up close
all the better to gape

oh this place, place, where no unboundary exists
everywhere junctions connections between this world
    and that
every passing on walkways and subways
and the border-guard peering into the still-open mouth

holes and dugouts and pores
through the skin of the country, these doors
through which passers-by
may not descend unauthorised
not a tear duct, nor a shallow well
but a mine in every hole
a deep long shaft
to where the canary *me* is held aloft

I teach straying from I, yet who can stray from me!
This *I* follows you from here until the hour of death
Throbs in your ears till you say 'Here *I* stands'

I do not say these things for a rouble or to fill up the time
    while I wait for a boat

(it is you talking, not I – I is your native tongue
tied in your mouth, in mine it began to wag)

while we sleep, *I* thinks about you

---

suburbangascompressionworks where the unstable
    sublimated mass
rises paraglides over paradise or over gas
the compressed is overgrown, but peonies grow
    abundant as the plucked

---

it is time to explain myself – let us stand up

earth cannot stand

she has no close or distant plans
no sense of her own rightness
she doesn't pity herself doesn't answer in answer to
doesn't lie down doesn't run
makes no particular mistakes
leaves no person without

earth opens her mouth but not to speak
nor does she stop herself being mired in herself

---

the intricate carved doors of the butterfly
don't flap forwards backwards so you
can pull your heart from its cavity
and peer on tiptoes over the garden wall

the suite of rooms won't sway or come apart,
nor will the mezzanine bend and snap
at last vision runs from the garden
says to reason: enough of your crap

and now in the whitest nights –
when light hardly catches its own –
our trial opens in court and takes flight
and marrow courses and teems in the bone

the prosecutor mops his damp brow
pours a thick glass with a hand that shakes
so water scatters in beads on the cloth
a tiny map of the Italian lakes

bone marrow, like porridge left overnight,
suddenly singing in full throat
a song of an old life, our old life,
but no more now than a flat joke

as if we weren't sawdust-stuffed, soap slivers,
splinters of worlds thrown into a pail
and the thick-lipped beer bottles
trumpeted our way

---

transparent pine legs flicker past
like a shadowy borodino battle
moscow like a played draught
slips out of reach   its draw is lateral

there: inseparable, clustered like grapes,
foaming goblets of lilac in the dark
caught in the thin smoke from war medals
mid-bloom, outwinging firework
not holy mother of god! not a dungeon!
but darkling glass in the entrance halls
v-sign smeared on the walls.
But I awoke and went   awol!

I saw the skull beneath the skin
its sockets its machined teeth its seam

not a bonnet but a bauble
the night sickblossom of a bluebottle crown

Trotting like guinea hens, Zulfiya
Zemfira, Maria and Russ*I*a
run like ink across the meadow
into the open maw of a severed head
roost on the perch in the mouth's red hollow

but I awoke before we were swallowed

---

the watery world is boiling and burning
its motors begin dully moving and turning
and dust in damp little scrupuli
coats the horse's muzzle and eye

who rides so late through standing water
it is the father, he holds his daughter
the cart rattles and clatters and shakes
but the child never wakes

hush now child don't be frightened
the sedge has withered from the lake
the heron calls, the stork has quietened
we'll get there in the time it takes

languor on the bosom, warm in the womb
It trembles like water in a manger
tell the child that the dawn has come
now the child's beyond danger

but deep in the rock where the sediment's hard
the underground water is born in the dark
and rises up the dungeon stairs
slowly up the legs of chairs

---

summarised
what was said
amounted to

she simply isn't able to speak for herself
so she is always ruled by others

because her history repeats and repeats itself
takes on ersatz and out of date forms

and there is no knowing where her quotes are from
nineteen thirty or nineteen seventy
they're all in there   pell-mell   all at once

not to remind us, you understand, just to plug the holes

(appalling really)

her raw material
her diamonds her dust tracks her dirt-coloured trailers
ancient forests mountain ranges
snow leopards desert roses gas flow
needed for global trade arrangements

her raw material doesn't want to do business with her
gives itself up without love will do as she wants

unclear what she needs

where's your *I*, where is it hidden?
why do strangers speak for you
or are you speaking
in the voices of scolds and cowards
get out of yourself
put that dictionary back on the shelf

she won't come out
it won't come right

look how ferry fleet she is
see her wings in aeroplansion
woolscouring steelbeating pasteurising
thousand-eyed thousand-bricked civic expansion
weavers singing at their non-functioning looms
voluntary wine-drinking zones
supre (forgive me lord) matists striding forth

junckerlords Kalashnikovs
bolshoiballet dancing out from behind the fire curtain
the fenced-in ghost of a murdered orchard

this[fucking]country
paradise sleeping in hell's embrace

---

let her stay like that, in bloom
I'll take my stand here
with the brief falling petals
with the night sentry

prostitutes pale shadows
under the shadows of trees on the arterial road
blinded by headlamps

approach the cars
careful like deer to the feeder

wagon-restaurant   plastic flowers
menu in gilded letters on leatherette
waitress with bitemarks on her neck

anyone who speaks as *I* can't yet speak

dust storm at the railway halt
where on another day we could have lit up a cigarette
the expanse of fields, rain-moist and restless
a retired officer in a military coat

a truck driver in his lit cabin, now we can see
whether it's high-walled like a palace's eaves
and whether light will dispel darkness between two tiny towns.

place your hand on my I and I will give way to desire

June 2014

From the Archive

Issue 152, July–August 2003

ELEANOR MARGOLIES

From a contribution of three poems
including 'From the Tate' and 'Cours
Belsunce: a Course in Good Sense'.
Fellow contributors to this issue
include Robert Saxton, Andrew
Motion, Monica Ferrell, Michael
Hamburger and Jane Weir.

JANUARY WEATHER

War moves on caterpillar tracks
as we sit fogbound, snowbound,
urging on the days of Janus.

You dream of ports frozen solid,
snow-deafened listening posts,
a high, pitiless Babylonian summer -

these would close the temple doors.
Salt and grit drive through the air,
and close beside you lies another's face.

Obiter Dicta

In memoriam George Fischer

FREDERIC RAPHAEL

1.

'Jewishness is, in the 20th century, a club from which there can be no resignations.' George Steiner's *pronunciamento* sounds compelling, but Jews are a discordant clan, prophets against kings, reform against orthodox, Zionists against assimilationists. Garrulous antagonism is their habitual style, anti-Semitism not unknown: Karl Marx called a rival socialist a 'yid'. The philosopher Berel Lang finds it offensive when people speak of *the* Jews, as if they formed a single, sinister bundle. The frequent use by broadcasters of 'the Jewish community' is a form of abstract ghettoization. Who speaks in that style of other citizens in an essentially secular society?

Greeks and Jews have in common that division is part of their strength. There were Greeks, as there were Jews, all around the ancient world, but no state called Greece until after the 1820's. Even in fissile ensemble, Jews lack numbers to command a reliable majority anywhere, including Israel. In the twenty-first century, those in the Diaspora are being called upon, especially from the Left, to dissociate themselves from 'the Jewish state'; they become admirable only by its condemnation. In symmetrical mode, 'the Palestinians' are divided from other Arabs and Muslims (who can wholly applaud Assad or the Iranian Ayatollahs?) and become innocent victims, always apt to be classified by the media as 'civilians', whatever rockets they fire, tunnels they dig.

In 1917, the British Foreign Secretary A.J. Balfour promised the traditionally vagrant race a 'national home' in Palestine. He feared, and over-estimated, their financial power more than he cherished their welfare. Apprehensive of a run on the pound, when the Great War was going badly, he allotted land that it was not his to people he did not care for. Territorial booty wrested from the Turks doubled as pay-off and dumping ground. An influx of Jews among the Arabs would serve the age-old imperial strategy of divide and rule, especially desirable, for British purposes, on the route to India, a single country that never existed until the East India Company was nationalised under the British crown. The sub-continent's holus bolus of Hindus, Buddhists and Muslims supplied the white man with another rich burden, the monotheist Sikhs his liege-men.

Furnishing common ground between one brand of subjects and another was no more Whitehall's imperial policy than it had been that of Rome. At the same time as Jews were being promised a small slice of the Ottoman empire, the British bribed Arab chieftains with tracts of land, kingly status, nominal autonomy. Only the migrant Bedouin declined to be pegged down with hand-outs. Opportunist sheiks got lucky with what seemed, at the time, miles and miles of fruitless sand.

T.E. Lawrence's wartime exploits against the Turks won him the title of 'Lawrence of Arabia'. He foresaw and feared that Britain's half-hearted Arab allies would enrich themselves on the oil the vainglorious western powers had allotted them to lord it over. He knew how much Whitehall gold had been needed to get them to mount brave camels and be eligible for royal imposture. When Lawrence applauded the idea of leavening the Levant with energetic Jewish immigrants, Rudyard Kipling wrote to warn him against being 'pro-Yid'. There were no Hebrew Gunga-Dins.

During the Sykes-Piquot resection of the Near East, as it was then called, the few thousands of surviving Assyrians were superfluous to the population of the fabricated kingdom of Iraq. The recalcitrant descendants of the biblical Babylonians were bombed into extinction when R.A.F. Bristol biplanes 'came down like the wolf on the fold', as Byron said of the ancient Assyrians. Arbitrary states, their corralled inhabitants riven by age-old antagonisms, were apt for ordering by the British and French. If often at odds, London and Paris were as one in building instability and corruption into the foundations of the new Near East. The French employed the previously despised Alawi tribe as their auxiliaries in Syria; the rise of the Assad tyranny a direct consequence.

Between the wars, the British established an Arab camel corps, under a seconded English general, Glubb Pasha, to be their surrogates in Transjordan, as it was then labelled. In 1948, when the Arabs united in seeking to abort Israel, at the end of the British mandate, Glubb led the Arab Legion across the natural barrier of the Jordan and advanced on Jerusalem. His success, amid Arab failure on other fronts, led to the deletion of 'Trans' from the Hashemite kingdom's title; its claim to the West Bank soon became immemorial. At the same time, Israel was recognised by the United Nations, reluctantly by the British and not for a long while by the Vatican. No harmonious, self-reliant democracies were encouraged anywhere in the region. Egypt remained a British fiefdom, as it had been Roman in the age of Augustus. In 1956, Glubb Pasha was relieved of his command. The Arab Legion became part of King Hussein's mostly Bedouin praetorian guard.

In 1919, U.S. President Woodrow Wilson's evangelistic notion of 'self-determination' had served to accelerate self-advancing political careerism in the place of disgraced hereditary monarchies. Both Austria-Hungary and the Ottomans had allowed a variety of people and races to co-exist in more or less peaceful patchwork. The assassin of the archduke Franz-Ferdinand had little loud support even in 1914 Serbia. Austria's deliberately unacceptable demands then precipitated a war that was intended to buttress its imperial power and ended with the Hapsburgs' humiliating eclipse.

The post-Great War map of eastern Europe and the Balkans, redrawn at Versailles, was ominous with papered cracks. Opportunist political factions soon coalesced in loud, street-fighting bundles, left and right. Ex-corporal Adolf Hitler was quick to enlist as Field Marshal Ludendorff's 'drummer'. Having played an ignominious part in the abortive right-wing 1923 Munich putsch (he is said to have fainted with fear when the police charged), Hitler made successful bid for leadership of the National Socialists by writing *Mein Kampf* (*My Struggle*) while in prison and by the entertaining antisemitic rant with which he filled Munich's beer halls. The promotion of the Big Lie was formulated in a compendium of self-glorification.

Mein Kampf did not mention that its author owed his Iron Cross to a Jewish captain whose runner he had been. Although he was in the front line, there is no evidence that Hitler, employed as a dutiful runner, ever did any fighting. During the following ten years, anti-Semitism became a loud and effective rallying call: Jews were what everyone else was distinct from. Windy Hegelian philosophising and paranoid fantasy supplied boosts for Germany's ruthless self-pity.

Woodrow Wilson's well-meaning plan for European pacification primed the defenestration of Jews from regions where they and their ancestors had, in many cases, lived for centuries. Official Christianity made no objection. The papal legate, Cardinal Pacelli (later Pope Pius XII) came to subservient terms with Hitler in 1933. As long as the Roman Catholic church survived, everyone else could go to hell, their likely destination in any event. Two years later, the synod of the Church of England passed a motion – the Archbishop of York the sole dissenter – in favour of denying German Jews sanctuary in Great Britain. Henry Ford and Father Coughlin led the call for the United States to close its gates to Semitic refugees. Joseph and Mary fared better in Bethlehem.

2.

In art, star signatures embellish and enrich the work. A lone intelligence can make impressive marks. Duplicity, rhetoric, illusion, fancy and wit generate marvels. Inspiring as some may find them, such works are never essential. The world has no need of Spinoza, Schoenberg, Proust and who all else in order to continue spinning and spawning. Jean-Baptiste Coffinhal, aptly named president of the 1794 tribunal that condemned Antoine Lavoisier to death on a spurious charge, is said to have justified the sentence by saying that the Revolution had no need of *savants*. Genius was dispensable.

Departures from the ordinary, in art, politics and business, may foster masterpieces; they also challenge received notions of how things are and embarrass the ideologist. The academic curriculum will survive on the second-rate. A.E. Housman spent his prime on a once and for all edition of Marcus Manilius' *Astronomica*, whom very few would choose to read, with or without its immaculate *apparatus criticus*. What example even of the finest art would a worldwide referendum elect to preserve if it entailed the suppression of Kleenex?

Greeks and Jews have always been liable to be labelled 'too clever by half'. Versatility, sublime or mercenary, may make them useful; it rarely makes them loved, even by each other. Ancestral loyalties and cryptic scripts render them suspect. What interpreter is entirely trusted by those who depend on his agile services? 'Science', by contrast, passes for an open, universal language. However difficult to follow or obscure its notation, it is without ironic nuance or metaphysical superstructure. As in chess, there are no hidden moves. This does nothing to promise that it is an easy game.

However obscure his speciality or daring his innovation, the scientist has a methodical obligation not to be wilfully false. Karl Popper argued that an honest researcher must seek, by all available means, to disprove his or her own theory. To suppress or ignore disconcerting data is the mundane equivalent of the sin against the Holy Ghost, the schoolboy version of which was 'pissing on the altar'. Spinoza's slogan *deus sive natura* implied that science was the new theism. The fetishistic Christian faith in the miraculous became, by definition, not merely questionable but self-contradictory.

While the Nazis' malevolent coinage 'Jewish science' is without genuine sense, ability to think outside the Christian box marks trail-blazing heterodoxy in intellectual as well as in artistic arenas. Roman Catholics are rare among Nobel prizewinning scientists. Heretics who think for themselves – Giordano Bruno an obvious example – are more likely to be original and to pay the price. Tycho Brahe, safe in Denmark, made a farce of Rome's official astronomy. The earth moved. The hierarchy refused to budge. *Eppure si muove...* Only when it became laughable to persist was Aristotle ditched; Christianity survived with the usual pontifical capacity for ruthless revision.

Wittgenstein made play with the puzzle of a caricature which looked like a duck through one eye, so to say, a rabbit through the other. It was, he implied, senseless to ask which was the image's 'real' meaning. Georg Simmel, Wittgenstein's senior by many years, was less arch: in his masterwork, *The Philosophy of Money* (1900), he argued that different readings came of recourse to different scales, in particular ethical as against economic. Nothing was definitively evaluated except in a selected context or a specified ambience. Values of all kinds were read into things, not inherent in them.

'Don't ask for the meaning, ask for the use' was how Wittgenstein put it. He was never more assimilated to *entre deux guerres* Cambridge than in eschewing any mention of money and in avoiding the first person singular. Freud was an occasional coffee-housing topic, self-analysis not. Grammar was the guardian of sense. Only in private, with Bertrand Russell, and in a tone of anguish, did Wittgenstein confess how he had concealed, perhaps from himself as well as from others, that his thought was 'one hundred percent Hebraic'. Practice trumped belief.

Post-1945 Oxford and Cambridge philosophers limited themselves to intellectual topography very different from what continental Europe's *philosophes,* a many times removed cousinage, took to be the heart of the matter. The old continent's surviving intellectuals thrashed about in search of a valid explanation of why their culture had caved in. They rarely put their own opportunism in the frame. *Mea culpa* was not a common plea, though it saved the pitiless and plausible Albert Speer's neck. It also served that he was 'a professional man', the architect of his own survival.

Shameless collaborators and *fascisants* intellectuals,

like the egregious (and bigamous) Paul de Man, shucked soiled colours and slipped into new, serviceable all-weather rig. De Man was quick to dismantle language of any kind of reliable moral grammar; nothing was right or wrong but opportunity made it so. Werner von Braun was easily translated to the U.S. where, like Archimedes in Syracuse, he wedded mathematics to weaponry. President Eisenhower warned of the consequences but did nothing to avert them. Nothing has been more profitable or unquestioned than the arms trade. It has arched diplomacy off the world's playing fields and rendered international relations without nuance or morals. Thou Shalt Kill is its sole commandment.

The Anglo-Saxon intelligentsia of the 1950s gloried in mundane empiricism. Logical propriety doubled with piecemeal problem solving. When did success need a theory? No metaphysical or systematic elaboration had a place in the patchy philosophising that Wittgenstein and his acolytes called 'The Game'. Who knows if Wittgenstein knew that prostitutes spoke of their activity in precisely the same terms? Betty Grable was his favourite film star.

The loudest iconoclastic objection to Oxbridge complacency was delivered in Ernest Gellner's *Words and Things* (1959). Gellner was both foreign and doubled as an anthropologist; it amused him to catalogue academic fauna with categorical mockery. Gilbert Ryle, mandarin editor of *Mind,* the house magazine of English philosophy's Oxbridge in-group, denied the outsider even a hostile review. Bertrand Russell was the angry old-timer who blew the whistle on the upstart Gellner's behalf. In his nineties, he again had the honour of being called a 'troublemaker'. Over forty years earlier, he had opposed British entry into the Great War and, after being docked of his Trinity fellowship for speaking freely, was sentenced to carpeted solitary confinement. Charlie Dunbar Broad, a colleague who did not greatly admire Russell's philosophy, was one of the few to oppose Bertie's ostracism, though many would welcome his return.

Ryle's chapter, in *The Concept of Mind* (1949), on 'The systematic elusiveness of I' declared that a person had 'no knowledge by acquaintance' of his own subjective self. In that light, the God Apollo's Delphic saying 'Know Thyself' took on the allure of an Olympian joke. Following Ryle's lead, Oxford philosophers derided sentences of the form 'I think that' as 'mere autobiography'. What Gertrude Stein said of Oakland, California – 'There's no there there' – became applicable to human individuality. Wittgenstein's gloss was hardly less cute: 'The subjective self is not an item in the book of the world.' Did the book of the world appear in the book of the world? Was there no danger of an eternal regress in making it so? Did it matter?

Ryle's eminent exegete William Lyons glosses him as meaning that 'I' cannot be observed by anyone. This fancy disappearing trick could well serve as a warrant for a cull of human beings who would have no entitlement to take it personally, since personality has no scientific status. The just robot, call it, in tribute to Kubrick's *2001,* Coffin Hal II, will cull superfluous life under the licence that any individual appeal against its logic must be insubstantial. Philosophy always risks underwriting what lies outside its field, murder scarcely the most unusual, if it served to enhance a career, as Martin Heidegger and Carl Schmitt were proud to illustrate, until they weren't. Both returned to academic eminence after the war. In carefully culled symposia, Heidegger would never answer any questions he had not previously vetted; he brooked no critical supplementaries. Arrogance promises the masochistic academic a happy outing.

In recent times, John Gray has argued, as if it were something new, against what he claims is the myth of integrated personality; we are all, he claims, ragbags. So? Were this true, or deemed so, we might as well, as Wittgenstein put it in another context, 'divide through' by what is universally the case and then resume our patchwork identity. Articulacy and contradiction are essential to the kind of analysis which Gray uses against the 'self'; spiders never argue and have not changed in millions of years.

All but alone among philosophers, Soren Kierkegaard (1813–55) stood out against what became the Marxist/Freudian/positivist depersonalisation of morals. Insisting on a man's sins being his own, he took individual salvation, resistance to temptation (including fathering children out of wedlock) to be the prime concern of a human being. During his lifetime no major war took place on European soil. The prospects for mundane personal freedom and civil negotiation between nations and classes would never be so good again.

3.

Jean-Paul Sartre's quick-off-the-mark 1944 benevolence regarding *les Juifs* owed more to sly apology for his and Simone de Beauvoir's wartime conduct than to his version of Kierkegaard's idiosyncratic creed and the existentialism of Martin Heidegger (the latter's brother maintained *Sein und Zeit* was Dada with a straight face). Sartre's indoor life as an inactive member of the Resistance, his HQ close to the stove in the Café de Flore, was at the false heart of his name-making, alibi-fashioning fictional tetralogy *Le Chemins de la Liberté,* of which the fourth volume remained pending. He had had no noticeable reluctance, in 1940, when he took the job, in a prestigious Parisian *Lycée,* of a forcibly evicted Jewish *professeur.*

After others, including what some might call a disproportionate number of Jews, had risked their lives in the Resistance, Sartre affected the authority of his fictional alter ego, Mathieu, a *résistant* not unlike Robert Jordan in Hemingway's *For Whom the Bell Tolls.* Sartre, for all his anti-Americanism, was also a disciple of John Dos Passos' narrative innovations. André Malraux, who had advised him to bide his time until the arrival of the British and Americans, emerged in the summer of 1944 dressed as a colonel and entitled, as a veteran flyer in the Spanish civil war, to take command of a group of Maquisards. He went through the motions of being in action in time to be eligible to become General de Gaulle's lieutenant and the literal cleaner of France's claim to cultural supremacy.

Playing the philosemite, Sartre declared that France's surviving Jews would be well-advised to resign themselves to never being healed to the common culture. Claude Lanzmann, his long-time follower, in the 'family' centred on *Les Temps Modernes*, had been active in the Resistance at the age of eighteen. Lanzmann's unparalleled film

Shoah was a belated assertion of Jewish pride and an implicit justification of Israel. Sartre chose not to endorse Israel for fear of offending Stalin; he was less cautious when it came to the intellectual assassination of Parisian rivals (Mauriac, Camus etc.).

In Poulou's brave renewed world, the Jew alone was denied existential choice; for reasons too immutable to fit his logical scheme, Jews had no alternative but to be what others said they were. The nostrum of universality could not, as Napoleon had assumed, immerse them in a secular baptism from which they might emerge indistinguishable from everyone else. They should forget any commonplace version of St Paul's undiscriminating heaven. Sartre's bossy advice (akin to '*vive la différence*') was better expressed by Mel Brooks in *The Producers*: 'If you've got it, flaunt it.'

How does a Jew in a post-Christian society, whatever his contribution to the common culture, unlatch himself from his stained shadow? Denial and revelation run in the same lane. As even Hegel conceded, accusingly, the Jew is elemental; his pride his flaw. While in Argentina, Adolf Eichmann once all but conceded the maddening priority of the Jew.

In a recent article, Slavoj Zizek's affectation of impartiality – indistinguishable from condescension – ignores this adhesive singularity. While seeking to rationalise the world's disapproval of how Israel treats the Palestinians, he shows no inclination to mock the selective moralists who ignore contemporary massacres of immeasurably greater scope and cruelty. Hundreds of thousands have been murdered and gassed in Syria, but who denounces 'the Arabs' or Islam? Zizek, like many other self-anointed thinkers, makes the 'guest' Jew the only species on perpetual probation. A vagrant life is what you deserve when you all voted to crucify God, even if you didn't.

The Jews' indelible delinquency purges Christianity's guilty conscience in filching their God and their scriptures. Anti-Semitism is best diagnosed not by the psychological biopsy of individual paranoids but by observing its use, by both solemn Christians and political ideologists. Even as Christian credulity wanes, its fading prospectus for salvation has to indicate some reason for its delay. The scapegoat Jew serves today's virtuous sects as he did St Augustine more than a thousand years ago and as Trotsky did Stalin more recently. The nigger is no longer in the woodpile, but Eliot's Jew is still liable to be underneath the lot.

Hence the outrage that he is not ashamed of lodging himself in that sliver of ancestral land from which his eviction would re-invigorate any number of myths, Islamic no less than Christian or Marxist. When the wandering Jew calls somewhere home, it at once challenges Christian dogma and punctures Moslems' belief that they are the favourites of Allah. Who but an Israeli with two feet on his own ground (and who happened to be a Nobel prize-winner) could hear an Englishman say, 'I don't usually like Jews, but I like you' and respond 'I usually like Englishmen, but I don't like you'?

4.

Patriotism, like religious practice, is often a fake antique. Although *Germania* is the title of a book by Tacitus, there was no page in the atlas for a unified 'Germany' before Bismarck's dragooning vanity put an end to Austria's lazy despotism. While we admire captains who go down with their ships and Spartans who hold the pass, we also glamorise the apostate, the scoundrel and the drop-out. For many, Tolstoy is but a great writer, Dostoyevsky the genius. Vladimir Nabokov, a closer reader of Russian than most translators or critics, rated Dostoyevsky a 'journalist' driven literally mad by the mock execution to which he was subjected by the Tsarist authorities. Nabokov's own beloved father was murdered by a communist assassin while addressing a meeting of exiles, in Berlin. Trotsky, who would suffer a similar fate, in Mexico City, called Nabokov *père* the cleverest of the 'Cadets' (centrist liberals).

Revolutionary and reactionary cleave to implacable ideology. The Jacobins' unquestionable praesidium is of a piece with Marx's dictatorship of the proletariat. There is no appeal against logic, honest or fabricated: buy the premise and you are committed to whitewashing the penthouse. Atheist grandson of a rabbi, Marx inverted Hegel's Idealism and preached, with much the same determinist logic, that human society has an inescapable destiny. Single-party politics ape the inhumanity of physics and the resistance-is-useless jealousy of Jehovah. Autocracy is a mundane form of monotheism and sings similar hymns: 'For the sake of Comrade Stalin, we drove the White Guards back...'

The philosopher Bernard Williams once deigned to instruct me that the Holocaust was morally no worse, merely more extensive, than massacres of earlier times. Must he be right? The machinery of National Socialism derived from the conjunction of religion's parody, ideology, with twentieth century technology. The mechanisation (and merchandising) of death, under hegemonic licence, altered the scope and denomination of murder and theft; quantity became quality, pillage just reward, murder duty. The higher executives of the Holocaust rarely did their own dirty work. Hundreds of thousands of ordinary Germans killed two or three million Jews, face to face, before mechanisation saved most of them from bad dreams and hastened the process. Logic required the killing of a million and a half children. Senior planners of the *Shoah*, especially those of elegant mien and fluent English, escaped judgement after the war.

William Lyons, emeritus professor of philosophy at Trinity College, Dublin, thinks Bernard Williams wrong: 'while the Holocaust certainly reached new levels of quantity in massacres, *it also plumbed the absolute moral depths in its execution* [my italics].' 'It was a long-planned and long-drawn-out programme of seeking to destroy a whole culture and heritage by...a uniquely evil logic that... led to its Q.E.D, "the final solution".' A starred first in complacency, Williams' assertive hauteur was the trademark of a brilliant career in Oxbridge formula one caucus racing.

Abdication from practical responsibility is typical of intellectuals such as Ezra Pound. T.S. Eliot, currently said to be Britain's favourite poet, knew how to lie low. He loved cats. The post-war whitewashing of Pound needs to be aired; not as a prelude to dragging his bones on a hurdle through the streets, but to illustrate the presumption of the clerisy (Frank Kermode's posh term) in delivering pardons. In 1949, Eliot's prestige swayed the committee into awarding the first Bollingen Prize to Ezra Pound, so applying a prime lick of whitewash on the engineers and sycophants of the Holocaust. Karl Shapiro, a good poet and wartime hero, blighted his prospects of featuring among the literary top dogs by loud refusal to applaud posh fascism.

The claim that metaphysics is essential to the exaltation of a work of art, as Kermode said, with D.H. Lawrence in mind, is used to justify soothsaying, on the grounds that masterpieces may come in its train. Academic aesthetes can propound a morality which arms Plato's suspicion that 'poetry' (the Greek *poiesis* embraces all the arts) distorts or derides eternal verities. Plato's *gennaion pseudos* (misleadingly translated as 'noble lie') postulated an analogy between 'natural law' and oligarchy based on rigged genetic precedent. As Popper had the nerve to declare in *The Open Society and its Enemies*, master-racism begins with refined intentions. Plato's charge that art can do no better than make a copy of a copy is either feeble or negligible; but to read him as an iconoclast who wanted no idols in the temple is to miss what he himself exemplified: the prophet, in evangelic mode, who uses 'nature' in a deceitful manner by appropriating Truth for tendentious purposes.

Never so rhetorical as when he denounced rhetoric, Plato's tactic was to deflect criticism from his own worldview. His deprecation of egotism is more pertinent when directed against dogmatic philosophy than as a warrant for the eviction of artists from his ideal *polis*. The preacher of almost every known faith, including faithlessness, affects privileged access to a singular Truth in order to validate one course and damn another. Many things are true; any militant claim to unique access to the Truth threatens to put men in bondage and tie dissenters to the stake.

In the view of what A.J. Ayer chose to call 'journeymen', as against 'pundits', philosophy cannot legitimately prescribe what can only be lived. More linesman than referee, the journeyman quizzes the logic of ethical theories; their construction is not his business. Except in circumstances of extreme common peril (a Roman dictator's term lasted only a strict six months), the conduct of a citizen is for him or, today, for her to determine. The democratic state is defined by preserving free access to the middle ground, never to prescribe what can be said in it. Intellectuals may advocate whatever course they choose; it is never their right to lay down the law. The ex-Communist Oxford pundit Iris Murdoch held that lying was always wrong. If, for example, she were asked by the Gestapo whether any Jews were hiding in the house, she said she would be obliged to tell them the truth. Exceptionless philosophy dips its pen in blood.

On the other hand? The loutish aggression (by neighbouring Croton) of the kind that destroyed hedonistic, inoffensive Sybaris in 510 B C looms often in human history. When were we ever short of prowling Midianites? The meta-Sybarite assumes that *laissez-faire* is so obviously the best form of civility that nothing rude will long disturb or displace it. In prosperous times, pluralistic society tolerates exotic flavours; in petty doses, they spice routine diet. A democracy is supposed to be robust enough to digest the nutritious, excrete the toxic. Spinoza, no marked optimist, said that the happy man does not think about death. Was he implying that revealed religion, with its morbid vanities, is an advertisement for death, and a licence for administering it? Is it not?

5.

Today, what Philip Bobbitt calls 'the mercantile state' peddles genteel pluralism while abrogating any right to enforce it or conceding seniority to reason. The element of show in the participation of royalty and notables in public ceremonies, especially under religious auspices, persuades the naïve that England, for eminent instance, is still a Christian country. Any crusading enthusiasm to institute Eliot's ideal state, purged of all but a few 'free-thinking Jews', would reveal how officious the pundit's modesty. His and Neville Chamberlain's favourite weapon was a rolled umbrella. If the Creed, any creed, however virtuous, were enforced with inquisitorial sanction, liberal society would be scuppered by its own lack of nerve.

The war waged against Sybaris by grim Croton (even today's Crotone is unusually charmless) towards the end of the sixth century B.C. was primed by Pythagoras and his dragooned, idealistic, vegetarian followers; they even eschewed kidney beans because of their anatomical form. Seeing other people happy brings out the ideologist's sword. As a young man Pythagoras fled the island of Samos after falling out with its enterprising tyrant Polycrates. He himself then evolved into the autocratic leader of a sect of bloodthirsty vegetarians who were, in time, spat out even by the Crotoniots whom they had inspired to victory. It is by no means certain that Pythagoras was the first to propound that the square on the hypotenuse was equivalent to the sum of the squares on the other two sides. He may have heard it from the Babylonians.

The reciprocity of tragedy and comedy in public theatre is emblematic of the duplicities and mood changes of an articulate state. By squaring off against each other, comic and tragic hold the ring and enliven the language. The static state which Plato imagined to be blessed with durability procures moral stagnation and tied tongues. The inflexible cannot bend; it can always crack. Any authority which labels its doctrine unquestionable deprives truth of meaning and elasticity. The Platonic model, soldered to Christianity, gave unique authority to a self-righteous state with a morality that promised salvation to the obedient, hell fire to those who dared to think for themselves.

Fear of freedom can be as great as desire for it. Sexual morality is a model for hopes, desires and apprehensions of all kinds: do I really want what I imagine I would like? The temptation to argue for private languages is liveliest in sexual fantasy. To express desires in words is liable to render them grotesque or comic. The conscious fantasist, keeping things to himself, can stay the far, or near, side of articulate and still be entertained by the unspeakable. The contradictions said by Marx to be unique to capitalism have complex sources. Did he recognise this, belatedly, in his happy-ever-after concept of the withering away of the state? A limited vocabulary without nuances, like Orwellian Newspeak, is central to such a fancy: the state of the language will then be coterminous with the language of the state.

Purposeful eagerness to bless communism with a long, as it were aristocratic, pedigree could be seen in George Thomson and V. Gordon Childe. Both Marxists of stimulating quality insisted that lack of differentiation of labour was typical of the classless state of primitive man. The use of 'state' confuses two senses and leads to a glib conclusion. Marxist mythology sought to prove and privilege an *ur*-economy which equated specialisation with deviance from the ideal. Every society subsequent to primitive communism could then be deemed an aberration. Only by eliminating the perverse could man be restored to a state in which he neither victimises others nor becomes their victim. In totalitarian politics, the promise is the evidence; scepticism sin. The second coming of a classless society would bring salvation on earth. Stalin's parody of the Inquisition destroyed millions of lives on the way.

Marx placarded his bearded ideas as scientific. His own academic studies had concentrated on the ancient world. Blithe credulity lay at the heart of his notion that the dictatorship of the proletariat, if inevitable, would be a passing phase. Eventually, whenever that might be, everyone would be liberated from dread; in the classless society, necessity and freedom would be synonymous: the state and its officers would become superfluous. In the world at the end of the red rainbow, Trotsky said, echoing the master, people would spend their time in uplifting activities, music in the broad Greek sense. The nicest thing about Marx is also the most alarming: he preached the bloody destruction of bourgeois society and its replacement by an earthly paradise on no better grounds than belief in the automatic machinery of destiny. The myth of a return forwards to the lost golden age promises salvation without Christ.

Can the dialectic ever arrive at a decisive conclusion? What bell will ring when the ultimate synthesis is reached? What would it be for humanity to disembark from the treadmill of contradiction onto a platform of perpetual harmony? It could occur only in an extra-terrestrial sanctuary. To argue against human perfectibility or in favour of it is logically impractical: all speech, except the word of God, is fissile. Roland Barthes makes the point with his concept of the infinite extensibility of the simplest phrase. Theology is *pi* in the sky.

6.

The tendency of intellectuals and/or false prophets is to crave a world in which they themselves would be docked of variety or, better, dock others of it. How is it that they dwell on their own punishment or disappearance? Albert Camus' 1945 question, why we should not commit suicide, has perennial significance. The intellectual, like the doctor, is liable to toy with his own destruction; what we ourselves control does not, supposedly, menace us. Killing oneself is a declaration of independence. As Seneca and Petronius proved, Romans had proud recourse to it if humiliation or torture loomed. Petronius had the *brio* to make a joke of his own terminal bath, red with his own slow blood. The word *suicidium* did not exist in classical Latin. Christianity's dog Latin made it a sin. For Cato the Younger, contriving his own death, with a rhetorical flourish, was a fitting gesture of disdain for Julius Caesar and a rejection of dictatorial *clementia*. How

should a true man agree to be pardoned for having done the right thing?

Jean-Paul Sartre's abhorrence from contingency echoes Freud's disgust with shit. It was not merely the *thinginess* of things which dismayed the pre-war author of *La Nausée*; it was also his own nothingness. The *Luftmensch* adds nothing indispensable to the world. The individual, *any* particular person, is at once the merchant of thought and irrelevant to any general statement about the universe.

In science no one says anything that might not, in principle, be said by another (in Darwin's case, for instance, it actually was). Science discounts or sequesters the singular instance. Nothing scientific can be posited about the unique; exceptions remind us of the rule but cannot furnish one. The ultimate case is the scientist himself: his name alone cannot certify his work as an artist's signature does his creation. Individual genius is superfluous to the logic of science, if not to its index. Here again the scientific affectations and confusions of the Marxists become manifest: the Party, for all its shifty devotion to heroic figures (who may at any time be expunged from the roster), is by definition wiser than the wisdom of any individual, however close he may have been to the genesis of the movement.

The question of whether Karl Marx was ever wrong is as rarely raised among the faithful as whether Jesus was at his divine best when he cursed the fruitless fig tree on the dry road to Jerusalem (in his native Galilee it would have been in season). No personal delinquency can damage the standing of the Party, just as no error by an individual (and *all* errors are, in a totalitarian context, committed by individuals) can overset the sublime rectitude of Christianity or Islam.

Religion's habitual self-validation is the basis of Kenneth Burke's smirking justification of Stalin's Moscow show trials: in Marxist logic, the system can never be 'guilty' when things go wrong, hence the accused must be. The Party and the Pope share premises. Readers of Amin Maalouf's *Le Naufrage des Civilisations* (2019) may notice that a Francophone Coptic Christian, now a French academician, can rate the Israeli victory in 1967 a kind of abomination, since the so-called *Naqbah* led to a loss of faith and face among the Arabs. He may not declare this out loud, but one hears the whisper. Any Jewish success abases the other monotheisms. What is unforgivable is less Israel's conduct towards actual people than its insolent victory over Islam and the consequent threat to the credulity of the masses.

When Roland Barthes speaks of the elimination of myth, following the dispossession of the bourgeoisie, he implies that language will no longer carry the possibility of 'going on holiday'. There will be no use for a pack of lies. He then concedes that such a purge is practically, if not logically, inconceivable. What language do they speak in heaven? What could there be to say when and where there is nothing more to be said? Perfection implies ineffable sterility.

Sartre's conceit and his sense of being superfluous *vont de pair*. He cannot keep quiet and yet he recognises his talkative irrelevance to the overthrow of the bourgeoisie. Whatever is inevitable will happen with or without the help of those who seek to advance it; any such move is literally inhuman. To call it 'necessary' is a Platonic play on words: what cannot, theoretically be avoided is blessed with an overtone of being morally desirable.

How could a 'humanist' (as an early Sartre pamphlet declared the existentialist to be) promote a political philosophy based on inhumanity? Heidegger supplied a distinguished case. Hegel's notion of Reason excluded any evidence that might blight his theory. Dogmas of inevitability license rulers to behave with programmatic heartlessness far beyond the appetite of the sadist or the capitalist. Barthes' restless interest in myth, however winsome its style, is of capital significance. Fundamentalism is often touted as a point of view unalloyed by liberal hypocrisy. In good times, it lies dormant; religious or quasi-religious conflicts ring its tocsin.

7.

The blood libel lies at the heart of the cleft between Christian and Jew. Nothing more clearly announces an unbridgeable gap between pseudo-species than the fact that one makes a meal of the other. If a Christian child's slaughter were indeed necessary for the Passover diet, however grotesque the recipe, then nothing could or should assimilate the Jew to those he would then have made a meal of. The absurdity of the charge cannot cancel its utility; forget the truth, notice the use: the myth of the diabolical Jew has licensed brutality at least since the first millennium after Christ. His failure to come again sanctified murderous antisemitism such as the massacre, in 1066 A.D,, of some six thousand Jews in Granada, where the Moorish Sultans relied on their diligence. The Alhambra, the red castle, was conceived and its construction supervised by a Jewish vizier and crowned the city known as Granada of the Jews. Much good it did them.

For mythical purposes, it does not matter who is labelled dangerous or pernicious, as long as someone is. The charge of killing God brands the Jew a beast never reliably domesticated: like Aeschylus' lion cub he cannot be trusted not to turn and rend those who have accommodated him. John Murray Cuddihy, a maverick Jesuit, was the principal author of *The Ordeal of Civility* (1974), which relied on the notion, civilly argued, that the Jews had to qualify by their good behaviour (and a show of scholarship) to pass muster in a culture bonded, in many ways, by dogmatic malice towards them. Those who survive a wanton massacre had better watch their asses. Baptism, Cuddihy implies, can provide the best visa to a kind of anonymity. In earlier centuries, only the contrary Quakers had earlier postulated the gentle conversion of the Jews as the necessary prelude to the Last Days.

The division between the savage and the civilised requires no evidence that one behaves more cruelly or less rationally than the other; it requires only that their purposes be dialectically at variance. Thesis precedes and procures the rocky stability of antithesis: no in without an out. "The savage" had little definite sense until it became a warrant, like 'terrorist', for treating people defined under that heading without trial or mercy. King Leopold of Belgium set the style by slaughtering millions of the black population of the Congo whose severed ears became a form of currency. Who now thinks ill of Belgians?

Converts to ancient civility had no obligation to worship strange gods or, generally speaking, to defer to native ones, although abusive denial of the Olympians outraged public opinion and procured the martyrdom which more than a few Christians craved. In twelfth century Cordoba, the so-called *Convivencia*, the triune live-and-let-live civility of Jew, Christian and Moor was ruptured by Christian fanatics who went to outrageous lengths to exasperate the ruling Sultan by behaving like pigs.

The notion of the noble savage had small sense until it became a literary trope. Tacitus' skittish portrayal of the Germans, like Montesquieu's of the Persians, set the style for sentimentalising the outlandish. Margaret Mead's *Coming of Age in Samoa* (1928) was, according to some critics, less a contribution to anthropology than evidence that 'natives' were quite capable of spoofing the patronising foreigner. Rousseau's version of savagery had less to do with anthropological verities than with the supposedly Edenic condition of mankind in general before the conceit of the 'civilised' gave rude meaning to the savage. If we read Rousseau as Claude Lévi-Strauss might, before the 'civilised' were on the warpath uncivilised man (the rural primitive) was not yet branded with the brutality which then excused his merciless treatment by those with manufactured weaponry. It has been argued that cannibalism was, in many cases, invented to supply a warrant for the mercilessness of colonisers. The British exterminated the original inhabitants of Tasmania to the last man, woman and child.

Hitler's blond beast is a perversion of Nietzsche's *ueberMensch*. Hijacked by the Nazis, the philosopher's superman had nothing in common with contemporary Germans, whom Nietzsche, however teasingly, rated inferior to Jews. The noble savage is not a distinct breed, but precisely indistinct. He belongs to a timeless time when the primitive was man's invariable form; the nobility attached to him by Rousseau has no meaning except by contrast with civilisation and its impersonal artillery. No savage kills at a distance. Martin Green dared to make dynamite, not culture, the defining superiority of so-called civilised man. What seemed a paradox is now a truism.

In Aeschylus's dramatic trilogy, the *Oresteia,* civil substitution of the negotiable for the inexorable is at the root of the pact between the state of Athens and the individual. The worship of blood, on the other hand, forbids a man to abandon the vendetta or to agree to a reconciliation that lames him, like Jacob's play-off with the angel. Faith has no room for compromise. Contemporary uneasiness is declared by the difficulty modern man has in creating peaceful heroes. Its now favourite form of cinematic fiction depends, like religious fanaticism, on endless planetary wars without polite resolution and with very little dialogue.

8.

The postulate of 'The Nation', with undeniable calls on loyalty, suggests how unglamorous many republics are. While we live in the even light of compromise and the conviction that between civilised people no belief is worth dying for, nothing is more absurd, or certain, than death. Yet our admiration is vested in the rebel, the outlaw, the recusant, the killer (the glamour of Special

Forces allows as much). States cannot rely on vegan foundations; men, in their mortality, have to believe, or at least hope, that in the final analysis something is worth dying for. The strains to be found in *Eumenides,* for which even Aeschylus could hardy find an anti-bathetic conclusion, are innate in modern society. If we embrace the vulgarisation of values, we choose to live in a pool that is all shallow end. When all have prizes, who has one worth having?

In a society without contradictions, justice is bound to be a branch of executive absolutism. It is here that Popper's assault on Plato packs its best punch. When Plato seeks to banish the artist, with his divisive and derisive ways, from the ideal state, he fails to observe (or care?) that there cannot be justice without a literature or without a casebook of judicial errors and a machinery for their correction. Only God, never His clergy, can be sure that the unquestionable and injustice are not accomplices.

The bourgeois state, with all its faults and secular preoccupations, is the vivid antithesis of theocratic infallibility. The author of the *Oresteia* implies that Gods and men should have better things to do than to pursue implacable grievances through the generations. The uncompromising cannot be better occupied than in the pursuit of blood. Neither casual kindness nor passionate love aborts the call for vengeance.

The vendetta ends only with the extirpation of the other. Nothing is less playful than the blood feud. Those exempt from its claims, embarrassed perhaps by squeamishness, have made modern myths out of those, whether in the Mafia, the Cretan mountains or the Middle East, who refuse to desert their malice. It is tempting to preserve some sentimental link with those who reject all accommodation. It needed a passionless god such as Athene to wish civility on the Furies. Their sullen compliance allows room for the audience's uneasy conscience when it buys *The Eumenides'* conclusion. If civilised society is impossible while the blood feud is privileged, its appeasement, by payment especially, has something boorishly bourgeois about it.

Who would prefer a world where vengeance assumes priority over all other social responsibilities? How seriously should the dead be taken? The questions persist behind humanity's historical obsession. Recording history is a form of necrology, just as 'news' in television journalism is often obituary. The dead weigh on the living; the living, conscious of the abyss, seek to procure sketchy survival in the memories and records of those who will outlive them. The scandal of homosexuality has something to do with the shame of inconsequential indulgence. Grandchildren are the nicest evidence of our persistence. They derive from our flesh, but they are not the direct result of our lust, hence our unambiguous relations with them; Marcel Proust's with his grandmother a paradigm. Hannah Arendt made the Jew and the homosexual alike in disjointing the comeliness of family trees.

The first leaf of every history book has been written in a mortuary; ancient Egypt is the evidence that no people has past or future without accommodating the dead. Society is ceaselessly involved with finding a balance between memory and forgetfulness. Memory is inverted presentiment. In ancient Egypt, provision for the pharaoh's remains became a preponderant cultural obsession. The dead enjoyed comforts denied the living; as in Christianity, the future became a happier tense than the present. The persistence of hieroglyphics, which could be read but not heard, suggests reluctance to sanction flexibility, the urge to process the past into instruction and entertainment in the present. Dread of being digested by the world, of losing individuality, is symbolised, to a morbid degree, by mummification and embalming. The will (playing on the future tense) of the dead imposed itself on the living; for those who could afford it, the present became a dress rehearsal for the future.

The pharaoh knew, though he might pretend otherwise, that he had only his temporal, temporary power in order to procure his future bliss; as soon as he was dead, he would be incapable of preventing the next ruler from appropriating his tomb. While the pharaohs claimed to be creating their own monuments, there was a long tradition of eviction and appropriation. The funeral games of the Greeks, with their prizes for youth and their celebrations of vitality, rewarded those who best proved their distinction from the dead. In the cultures of both Greece and Egypt, the disposal of a famous corpse was crucial in the regulation of priorities. The orientation of society, in linguistic and architectural terms, digests the dead. An excess of respect reserves the future tense for the speculative and theological rehearsal of life beyond the tomb. A lack of it makes all 'sacrifice' without significance. Metaphysics and scripture become sacerdotal preserves denied to the politician. Nothing is less true of the Egyptian than Aristotle's defining characteristic of man; ancient Egypt's theocratic necrology had no public place, no middle ground.

The age of specialisation tends to make all overviews specious, but without them we proceed to a world walled with discreet academic enclosures. The public language is left to generalisers with axes to grind or bells to ring. In this way there is a risk of regression to Egyptian ossification without its exquisite memorials. It is, by the way, nice that post-pharaonic Alexandria became a centre for both armaments technology and literature, a hybridisation of Jewish, Greek and Egyptian arts. The passivity of Cavafy's civilised society in *The Barbarians Are Coming*, the citizens' appetite for their own humiliation, is an acknowledgement of the divorce between intelligence and the muscle exercised to defend values as well as goods. When we elect to leave the future to take care of itself, the Barbarians are us.

The Auras

GWYNETH LEWIS

Someone has threaded a string of beads,
using a needle and white-hot wire, tugged
through my optic nerve, to make
a pulsating necklace. Light rides
the Big Bang towards me, wielding a knife
of cauterising pain, its blade
one photon wide, precise.

    *   *   *

Ninth migraine this month. In my cave
I cower from noon's brain-piercing light.

I'm Eve, cover my face to blot
out the angel's laser sword. But I've seen
such sights.

    *   *   *

That rogue, Robert Graves, located
the floating islands of Celtic legend
in the brain of a migraineur. Atlantis explodes; that flash
in the visual cortex's pan is Avalon. A privilege?
No, a brain malfunction.

    *   *   *

Turn the world down, it hurts. Route 125
runs through my cranium. A Harley purrs
ten miles away; trucks roar,
bear down on me from the Gap. Roadkill,
I'm waiting for the coup de grâce.

    *   *   *

A windless wood. Greenery strobes,
leaf shade jazzes. Then there's that stem
rowing a private breeze, anomalous. There!
Can't you see it? Oh, super-
sensitive
me.

    *   *   *

Ice Halo™
Wearable Ice Pack for Migraine!

Put it on front to back. Fasten hook and loop...
Fuggeddit. Can't even see. I'm a blur in the mirror:
A man in a turban, William Cowper, poor soul,
Before he went mad. *Is that kohl
round your eyes?* No, pain. It's my Bedouin
look. *And the yashmak?* For the coming storm
of ground glass, each sliver
a prism of flaying sun.

    *   *   *

Are those mice in the rafters, or a fountain pen
scratching on paper? In the dark come the visiting dead:
William Blake, commanded by angels, complains
That words skitter away. Whitman is kind and Emily Dickinson
Knows the electrical termites.

Give me moths
For eyelids, or a world
I can bear. Please
stop now, I'm tired, no
please go on

    *   *   *

Number nineteen. Eyes covered, I play
Blindman's Buff, guess at the world. That's Suzanne
taking the puppy out; the bin man's buggy and that,
Ladies and Gentlemen, is the Hermit Thrush,
a blacksmith at her forge, unmaking the chainmail
that covers her breast,
link by unbearably heavy link.

    *   *   *

With the next aura, before pain arrives,
will you drive me over the Gap, up the Mad
River Valley, to the Bobbin Mill cascade,
and lead me to that unlit pool before
the sun reaches it, push me in and under the bone-
aching chute, so I rise, Madonna in white-lace mantilla
inside the falls, comforted, at last, with cold?

Writing in a Time of Violence

Padraic Fiacc's Demotic Aesthetic

Siobhan Campbell

IN THE WORK OF PADRAIC FIACC, the Belfast-based poet who died on January 21st of last year, there's both a reach for the sublime and a sense of what might easily destroy that yearning. Perhaps his education in Catholic schools in New York, as well as a brief stint studying theology, informs that sense of sadness at despoiled religious feeling and the consequent loss of potential for the visionary. The ambivalences and oddities of Belfast city are nearly always present, sometimes allowing for moments of lightness where the closed-in feeling opens up, suddenly, to something else:

> Low clouds, yellow in a mist wind,
> on far-off Ards,
> Drift hazily...
>
> I was born on such a morning
> Smelling of the Bone Yards
>
> The smoking chimneys over the slate roof tops
> The wayward storm birds
> And to the east where morning is, the sea
> to the west where evening is, the sea
>   ('First Movement')

Characteristic of his oeuvre though are poems where both language itself and the construction of the poetic line are at issue. A favourite device is to subvert reader expectations of the line and to abuse syntax for effect. Normal narrative associations are peppered with odd swerves, often using sentences stripped of pronouns. Fiacc likes to scramble word order and variously deploys ellipsis, disrupted cadence, sharp enjambments and an odd use of capital letters. This almost anti-musical approach gives the work a sense of belonging to the wider modernist movement while the socially engaged and apparently shocked conscience gives a sense of the distinctive place of the Northern Irish conflict as the main driver of these poems.

But this work is in danger of not receiving a full critical reading. Part of the reason may be the controversy over Fiacc's 1974 anthology The Wearing of the Black: an Anthology of Contemporary Ulster Poetry which divided opinion on the proper approach for poetry to social conflict. Fellow poet James Simmons' review of this work in The Honest Ulsterman took Fiacc to task for opportunism in presenting work from, to use Fiacc's phrase, poets who had been 'touched by violence'.[1] But Fiacc, as editor, clearly states that he wants the work to pose 'the question' about how a poet reacts to conflict and for poets to suggest 'how they have tried to come to terms with it in their poetry.'[2] As in his own work, he is interested in testing what forms, phrasing and poetic devices most fully meet the challenge. Fiacc approaches the aesthetic question in several different ways, and though not consistently successful (who is?), there is always a distinct sense of the poet grappling with the question of how to make art that has social purchase in difficult times.

Padraic Fiacc (known as Joe) was born Patrick Joseph O'Connor in Belfast in 1924 but spent much of his early life in New York. He returned permanently to Belfast, which he sometimes terms 'Hellfast', in 1956. The return marked a turn in the poems from the Celtic motifs of early sequences to work that twinned personal psychic distress with the social and political reality around him. Illustrative of his poetic debates is 'The Wrong Ones', from the 1977 Blackstaff Press volume, *Nights in the bad place* (also appearing in Ruined Pages, the invaluable 1994 selected poems edited by Gerald Dawe and Aodán Mac Pólin, now reprinted by Lagan Press).

The Wrong Ones

> The howl of the rain beating on the military tin
> Roof is like the tolling of a bell
> Tolling for a childhood more
> Murdering than murdered.
>
> I rise and stalk across the scarred with storm
> -erected daisies, night in the north, grass.
>
> My water-coloured twilit-childhood island
> -scape is barricaded with circles of rain-rusted
> Orange, coiled to kill, barbed wire.
>
> Behind the corrugated iron walls of the barracks
> Dead mother rises again to bang bin-lids
> On dark mornings to warn husband and sons
> 'The Pigs, the Pigs are coming!'
>
> The air is filled with shooting, the sky,
> The colour of smoke, wends across the soot
> -stained grass, the grey Belfast wind
> Is blowing against the unblooming-as-yet-wall
> -flower mind. I reach my hand out and touch
> Two-hundred-years-old iron and chipped brick.
>
> I'll be a 'son of a gun' for ever now.
> For ever now I'll never be right. I'm one
> Of the Wrong Ones.
>
>   No one will help
> The rubber-bullet-collecting kids.
> No one will help the grim-
> faced teenaged British soldiers or young
> Cops, hating the being hated.
>   We all
> Go down the road now sharp and small
>   As razor blades...
> I pick my steps across

My backstreet childhood as a soldier would pick
His steps across a little mine-filled field.

With the title suggesting that if a set of people are marked as 'wrong', they can never be made right, the opening introduces the military barracks, a normal part of the cityscapes of Northern Ireland. The 'childhood' is characterised as more active than passive, more 'murdering' than 'murdered', with the gerund implying that its effects continue to be negative. Such a childhood continuing into adulthood might feel like a living hell of missed opportunity and thwarted potential, and these motifs become key tropes in Fiacc's work.

From the second stanza, Fiacc's stretching and breaking of syntax is on display: 'I rise and stalk across the scarred with storm/-erected daisies, night in the north, grass.' The nod to Yeats ('I will arise and go now') may be invoked to imply a possible opposite to this 'scarred' landscape. Unpicking the syntax, it can be read both that the daisies are 'scarred with storm' and that they have been 'storm-erected'. The line-break, drawing attention to '-erected' implies something quite unnatural, not associated with daisies. The line without sub-clauses is 'I rise and stalk across the grass' but the feeling of the whole is dissociative even though the words appear to associate together well as, in the dark, one may have to 'stalk' and one may indeed walk over the flowers of weeds. The device of converging thoughts, using syntax to amplify their complexity, is also used in stanza three where 'Orange', a political word in Northern Ireland, is the colour of rusted barbed wire 'coiled to kill' in a sentence which syntactically can be read to convey that the 'childhood island-scape' (a childhood of the inner mind perhaps) is also 'coiled to kill'. This state, often portrayed by Fiacc as delusional and tormented is 'water-coloured', possibly difficult to see within, like 'twilight', with the latter also referencing the Irish revivalist tendency (sometimes called the Celtic Twilight) and its inbuilt idea of shading in or fading out. This 'twilight' is now a ' – scape', a psychological territory as well as a real one, and 'barricaded', though it is not clear whether barricaded in or barricaded to keep something out.

In just the first three stanzas, Fiacc uses several of the devices which permeate his work. It is as if the artistic space of poem is consistently invaded by the realities at play in society. The reaction of the poet to the psychological pressure of those brutal realities makes him develop a poetics of disruption and odd juxtapositions which force the reader to read in different ways in order to appreciate the set of possible meanings even while the idea of 'meaning' itself may be being upended. Here too is a vision of the natural world which reflects rather than offsets the psychic distress. From 'The howl of the rain' in the first stanza, to the air that is filled with shooting, making the sky 'The colour of smoke', there is image after image of this 'island/-scape' as being, in essence, 'unblooming', as the poet has it here. Here there is no salve, as the natural world sometimes provides for Irish poets.

Throughout the poem, and endemic in Fiacc, jaggedly broken lines and surprising enjambment convey a 'wrongness' that still contains an abject human connectedness. Fiacc considers the fate of not only the 'I', but also the 'rubber-bullet-collecting kids' whom no-one will help as well as 'the 'grim/ faced teenaged British soldiers or young/ Cops, hating the being hated.' The move toward a horizon which widens away from the protagonist's vision and which engages beyond the arena of one sector's experience is characteristic. Here, he shows a particular empathy for youths who have joined the British army or the police and who are young enough to have the innocence of those who hate to be hated. The poignancy of the idea of wasted lives works because it is in juxtaposition to the previous descriptions of bleak and inhospitable elements of the lived life. While the reader might have understood this awfulness to be particular to one 'side' of the conflict and therefore possibly politically motivated or aligned, Fiacc subverts any expectation of this, ensuring that the reader understands the nature of the 'all' as in 'We all/Go down the road now sharp and small/ As razor blades...'. In a move now seen as typical, 'razor-blades' may act as a qualifying adjective describing the people here invoked as well as acting as qualifier to the 'road' which is denoted as difficult and indeed, as bladed.

'Difficulty' is a word that applies to Fiacc in that the poetry is not easy to read, either syntactically, politically, or in terms of the sometimes brutal nature of the content. It is to be hoped that future readers will place this work in the light of the wider modernist project, something we have not been good at doing in Irish letters. Gerald Dawe and Aidan Tynan however, are part of this re-reading. Tynan, in his article on paradox and violence in Fiacc, draws on the work of Paul Celan, which is, he says, 'concerned not simply with the relationship between violence as a historical phenomenon and poetry as a means of representing experience but with how language itself, to the extent that it manifests an indelible inscriptive power, can be understood as containing an irreducibly violent component.'[3] And Fiacc himself had some sense of how his own work meets the psychic pressure on a poet in a contested social milieu. In a poem like 'Glass Grass', Fiacc elucidates a sense of the futility of the poetic impulse within a broken society. The poet is on his way out to a poetry reading and the poem opens with the 'scorched-cloth smell of burnt flesh', a left-over from that morning, 'a bomb in one of the parked cars'. The almost casual description is accompanied by dyspeptic images of the natural environment, the gulls 'glinting like ice on asphalt' and 'The sun, in a smog of cheap petrol exhaust/ Fumes:'. Where some readers might abhor the seeming matter-of-factness here, Fiacc often works with a kind of mock-innocence of reportage which allows the actuality of incident into the poem in a stark fashion, operating as a shock tactic. In the poem, the poet is on the move and the poem follows, 'Crossing the shadow-deflected town that burns,/ Crossing the always-takes, never-gives man'. The crux of the poem is the description of the city, where the poet has to duck flying glass on his way to the reading, and that of the reading itself where the poet finds himself 'Tired of trying to pretend I am not this

---

3 Aidan Tynan, 'A season in hell: paradox and violence in the poetry of Padraic Fiacc', *Irish University Review*, Vol.44, No. 2 (2014): pp. 341-356.

frightening / Freak…'. The poem builds to the dramatic moment when as part of interactions at the discussion, the poet lies, saying he cannot put himself into the mind of the man who kills. But his private horror is that he can do this: 'But I can, I'm polluted/With the poison of violence, born and bred into it.' He quotes his critics who call his poems 'cryptic, crude, dis/-tasteful, brutal savage, bitter…' and it's a moment of aesthetic wonder to the speaker that he finds himself on the wrong side of their argument. By the end of this poem, the reader feels that he may even equate his experience with that of the city itself where 'Belfast is a beaten sexless dog, hushed,/ Waiting for when or where the next blow/ Will fall.' The poem seems to convey that what is cryptic, crude and distasteful should indeed end up in poems as otherwise it causes writers to 'pretend'. The powerful disconnect described in this poem can be seen to be what drives the aesthetic that Fiacc develops throughout his work. In 'Glass Grass', what's at stake in terms of the role of publicly-facing poet is clear and it underscores why Fiacc might have perfected that tonal playfulness of the demotic and the ironic threading through his work. Such tonal play allows for the visceral disconnects to be felt within the fabric of the poem itself while simultaneously pointing to the other 'event' of the poem, that of what is happening outside and around it.

Critics of Fiacc have variously upbraided him for allowing the poem to be tainted with the actualities of violence but some also agree with Terence Brown that Fiacc captures 'unending psychic pain'.[4] Brown praises Fiacc for confronting anguish 'directly with moral and aesthetic courage' while others such as Fred Johnston and Brendan Hamill have noted the Blakean connection in Fiacc – responding, I take it, both to the fact that Blake believed the human imagination was born from conflict and to the dialectic approach taken by Blake and mirrored in pieces by Fiacc. As Johnston says, 'sometime in the future we may come to understand Fiacc as one of our most modern poets, his work transcending local politics yet grounded in a deep and very Northern – and urban – significance. We need to hear more of him; we need the occasionally chilling newness of his Belfast Blakean voice.'[5]

If the problem for some critics is that the violence in Fiacc's poetry is untransformed, is too much lodged in reality instead of being made to act symbolically, then they may be missing two things. One is the aesthetic choice made by Fiacc to write against the received metrical line, to instead use unsettling, shifty rhythms and surprising turns of viewpoint and address. They may also be missing the moralist impulse in this poet who seems to wail 'never again' in his descriptions of brutality. The sense of moral orphaning in Fiacc may also be lamenting the impossibility of the transcendent. The poems themselves may be saying that to speak of awfulness is better than not to do so, even if this form of art is itself open to interpretation as a 'violence' of the mind. All of this implies that Fiacc deserves more serious reading, and now especially because of his ability to portray the physical world as reflective of shifts of power among those who shout loudest. Against this, Fiacc provides a kind of dogged poetic resistance in his determination to write directly, and with feeling, from an unsettled and unsettling social and political milieu.

4 Terence Brown, 'Pádraic Fiacc, The Bleeding Bough', in *Northern Voices, Poets from Ulster* (Dublin: Gill & Macmillan, 1975), pp. 141–48. 'To be Irish in By the Black Stream is to know a permanent condition of loss; in Odour of Blood it is to know unending psychic pain.' p. 148.
5 Johnston, Fred, 'A poet of Blakean wrath', *Irish Times*, 8 Feb. 1997

'Reborn'

DAVID HERMAN

Benjamin Moser, *Sontag: Her Life* (Allen Lane), £30

SUSAN SONTAG always managed to find a ringside seat at the key moments of her time. Like Woody Allen's Zelig, she always seemed to be where the action was. In the late 1950s she was in Paris during the heyday of the new cinema of Godard and Truffaut. She was back in New York in the early 1960s, writing about Happenings, Merce Cunningham and John Cage. In the late Sixties, at the highpoint of the New Left, she travelled to Hanoi and Cuba. In the Seventies she debated Feminism with Norman Mailer and Germaine Greer. In the Reagan years she denounced communism and in the new eighties' celebrity culture, she appeared on the cover of *Vanity Fair*. During the siege of Sarajevo, she was there directing *Waiting for Godot* and she responded to 9/11 with a controversial article for *The New York Times*.

This was Sontag the public intellectual. However, the new biography by Benjamin Moser shows how little was known of the private person. This new Sontag was a woman often overwhelmed by depression, loneliness and a lifelong fear of death.

'All my life,' she wrote, 'I have been thinking about death...' Her second novel was called *Death Kit* and ends in an ossuary. Her best-known play was about Alice James who died of cancer. In perhaps her best book of essays, *Under the Sign of Saturn*, five of the seven essays are about dead subjects. In her later, darker work, during the 1980s and 1990s, she was drawn again and again to dead men, including Roland Barthes, Robert Maplethorpe, Walter Benjamin and Elias Canetti. In 1995 she told an interviewer from *The Paris Review*, 'most of the essays I've succumbed to writing in the past fifteen years are requiems or tributes.' Perhaps this was what drew her to WG Sebald. She called her essay on him, 'A Mind in Mourning'.

'She was an inveterate visitor of cemeteries,' her son wrote in his memoir, *Swimming in a Sea of Death* (2008) and in 1972 she wrote in her diary about writing an 'Essay on cemeteries (or film?)'. 'I prance around cemeteries all over the world,' she wrote the following year, '– gleeful, fascinated...'

Her father, Jack Rosenblatt, died when she was five. He barely appears in Moser's biography. Unlike her mother. There are few positive references to Mildred Rosenblatt. 'My mother lay in bed until four every afternoon in an alcoholic stupor, the blinds on the bedroom window firmly closed.' 'Tired all the time. Was she drinking + taking pills then?' 'I didn't feel, deep down, my mother ever *liked* me. How could she? She didn't "see" me.'

Sontag's childhood reads like the beginning of *Jane Eyre*. A sad, unloved child who doesn't fit into an apparently indifferent family. Her only sanctuary is her reading. 'When a small child', she wrote, 'I felt abandoned and unloved.' 'And shortly after I must have started hiding, making sure they *couldn't* see me... Always (?) this feeling of being "too much" for them – a creature from another planet...'

'The nailbiting,' she wrote, 'started at camp.' Asthma, a year later. Illness was perhaps her great subject. She wrote one famous book about illness, a fine essay about AIDS, and was often drawn to female invalids – Alice James, bedbound, with hysteria then cancer, and Simone Weil. The asthma led her mother and stepfather (Army Air Corps Captain Nathan Sontag, another absent, elusive figure in Moser's book) to move to Arizona and then southern California. 'At high school,' she once said, 'I used to buy *Partisan Review* at a newsstand at Hollywood & Vine and read Lionel Trilling and Harold Rosenberg and Hannah Arendt.'

In 1949, she visited Thomas Mann in Pacific Palisades. She was always precocious. In 1995 she told *Paris Review*, 'I remember reading real books – biographies, travel books – when I was about six. And then free fall into Poe and Shakespeare and Dickens and the Brontë's and Victor Hugo and Schopenhauer and Pater, and so on. I got through my childhood in a delirium of literary exaltations.' By 1947, barely in her teens, she is reading Spender's translation of Rilke's *The Duino Elegies,* Gide, *The Magic Mountain* ('the finest novel I've ever read', she wrote a year later), Romain Rolland's *Jean-Christophe*. A year after that she graduated from North Hollywood High School and left home.

Sontag was a student for most of the 1950s. First, Berkeley, then Chicago and Harvard, Oxford and Paris. She was only at Berkeley for one semester. She was barely sixteen. It was, she wrote, 'The beginning of real life.' In May 1949 she wrote, 'I AM REBORN IN THE TIME RETOLD IN THIS NOTEBOOK.' 'Everything begins from now – *I am reborn*.' The word 'reborn' is crucial. What follows over the next ten years are two attempts to create herself anew: sexually and intellectually.

Perhaps the most striking revelation in *Reborn*, the first volume of her diaries, and now in Moser's biography, is the account of her homosexual life in San Francisco in spring 1949, in bohemian Paris a decade later and then in New York. In the Preface to *Reborn*, her son David Rieff writes, 'she avoided to the extent she could, without denying it, any discussion of her own homosexuality...'. Many could not forgive this reticence. Moser finds it unforgivable, especially in the chapter on AIDS. 'AIDS sparked a revolution,' he writes. 'But it would be a revolution that Sontag would largely sit out: unable to speak certain words.' He criticises her story, *The Way We Live Now* (1986), because it 'was not about AIDS.' It 'was published into a context in which it was essential to name names – particularly the name of AIDS', and she didn't. He praises plays and novels about AIDS, 'united by sheer heartbreak'. Beside them, he writes, 'Sontag's contribution seems thin, dainty, detached.'

In 1949, after Berkeley, Sontag transferred to Chicago. A year later, in 1950, she met 'a thin, heavy-thighed, balding man who talked and talked, snobbishly, bookishly, and called me "Sweet". After a few days passed, I married him'. Philip Rieff was a sociology instructor at Chicago. In January 1951 she wrote, 'I marry Philip with full consciousness + fear of my will toward self-destructiveness.' It is the only journal entry for that year. There are no entries for 1952. Only a handful for the next three years. David Rieff, born in 1952, writes of her 'impossible marriage to my father...'. In 1979, Sontag, now in her mid-forties, at the height of her fame, heard various accounts of her ex-husband's Trilling lecture at Columbia University. It was called, 'Homage to Mr. Casaubon'.

In 1957 she left Rieff and escaped to Oxford, then Paris. This was her second, crucial rebirth. In Paris she found her voice as a writer. It was a key moment in French culture. In a book on Sontag, Sohnya Sayres writes:

> Bataille was still alive; Klossowski active... Cioran had published *The Temptation to Exist* in 1956; Butor's novel *La Modification* received the Prix Renaudot in 1957; Robbe-Grillet had finished *The Erasers*, *The Voyeur*, *Jealousy* and had begun writing his essays on the new novel. Sarraute was discussed... In film Bresson was already well known; Resnais, Truffaut, Godard part of the renaissance.[1]

The impact was dramatic on a young woman away for the first time from 1950s America. Immediately she started writing in her journals about bohemians and 'camp tastes', pornography, Artaud and de Sade. She fell in love with film and modern theatre ('Pirandello, Brecht, Genet – for all three ... the subject of the theatre is – the theatre', 21 February 1958). A few days later, she met Sartre and heard Simone de Beauvoir talk on the novel at the Sorbonne. She went to 'the [Cafe] Flore' and the Deux Magots.

This gave her much of the intellectual capital she lived on, back in New York, in the early Sixties. She was one of the critics who introduced the French intellectual avant-garde to America. Three features were immediately apparent in her early writing. First, her love of the essay. It was a form perfectly suited to her range of interests and the speed with which she picked up ideas. Secondly, she was a great enthusiast. 'I wrote as an enthusiast and a partisan,' she wrote in the Preface to *Against Interpretation*. And, finally, she was a Europhile.

Above all, she caught the spirit of the times. 'There were new permissions in the air,' she later wrote in *Where The Stress Falls*, 'and old hierarchies had become ripe for toppling... I saw myself as a newly minted warrior in a very old battle: against philistinism, against ethical and aesthetic shallowness and indifference.'[2] She went on, 'I thought it normal that there be new masterpieces every month – above all in the form of movies and dance events, but also in the fringe theatre world, in galleries and improvised art spaces, in the writings of certain poets and other, less easily classifiable writers of prose. Maybe I *was* riding a wave.'[3] 'Artists were insolent again, as they'd

been after World War I until the rise of fascism. The modern was still a vibrant idea...'[4]

When she died, Christopher Hitchens wrote, 'By the middle 1960s, someone was surely going to say something worth noticing about the energy and vitality of American popular culture. And it probably wasn't going to be any of the graying manes of the old Partisan Review gang.'[5] 'She was,' wrote Cynthia Ozick, 'the tone of the times, she was the muse of the age...'[6]

Television producers and magazine editors took to her. She was young, barely thirty when her famous essay, 'Notes on Camp', appeared. In her BBC documentary about Philip Johnson she appears in sunglasses, driving a sports car through Manhattan, the new cultural capital of the west. Unlike middle-aged men like Irving Howe and Lionel Trilling (and Philip Rieff) grumbling about the Sixties, she loved them. She sensed something new and exciting was happening.

The Sixties was her time. She met Warhol and Jackie Kennedy and was photographed by Diane Arbus. She had affairs with Jasper Johns, Robert Kennedy and Warren Beatty. In 1965 she was spotted at a posh Manhattan restaurant having dinner with Leonard Bernstein, Richard Avedon, William Styron and Jackie Kennedy. A friend describes a party: 'Edmund Wilson was there, and Susan Sontag was there, and Malamud was there, and Lillian Hellman was there.'

Her journals are full of references to 'the new sensibility'. The 'Spirit of the age is being cool, dehumanized, play, sensation, apolitical', she wrote. Her journals show how she tried to work out what was so distinctive about the new culture of 1960s New York: 'New way – Rauschenberg, Johns – is through literalness', 'most of the interesting art of our time *is* boring. Jasper Johns is boring, Beckett is boring, Robbe-Grillet is boring.'

What runs through these pages is her appetite for new experiences. In 1961 she drew up a list of the films she had seen recently. It goes on for over four pages. Von Sternberg and Pabst, Bergman and Kubrick, *Casablanca* and *L'avventura*. She started publishing essays and reviews for *Partisan Review*, the *New York Review of Books*, *The Nation* and *Commentary*. Essays on Simone Weil, Camus and Lévi-Strauss. In 1966, *Against Interpretation* was published.

Her journals show a young person in overdrive. 'The two great living writers, Borges and Beckett.' (10 September 1966) '[Walter] Benjamin is neither a literary critic nor philosopher but an atheist theologian practicing his hermeneutical skills on culture.' (12 November 1976) 'The Russians didn't have an 18th century.' (20 September 1977) 'Notional Rome in Shakespeare...' (12 August 1978) '[U]se of American vernacular movement (from Mack Sennett comedy, Fred Astaire, black disco dancers), of American energy.' (25 February 1979)

The range is typical. What is striking is her European canon. Europe was her cultural home from the visit to Thomas Mann in 1949 and her time in Paris to her love

---

1 Sohnya Sayres, *Susan Sontag: The Elegiac Modernist* (Routledge, 1990), p.31.
2 Susan Sontag, *Where the Stress Falls: Essays* (NY: Farrar, Straus & Giroux, 2001), p.269.
3 *ibid*.

4 *ibid*, p.271.
5 Christopher Hitchens, *Slate*, 29.12.04.
6 Cynthia Ozick, 'On Discord and Desire', 2006, republished in *The Din in the Head*, 2006.

for Bergman, Canetti and Benjamin. 'No American writer of her generation,' writes David Rieff in the Preface to *Reborn*, 'was more associated with European tastes than was my mother.' '*The Magic Mountain*,' she wrote when she was fifteen, 'is a book for all of one's life.' In 1953, in a bookstore in Cambridge, she opens a volume of Kafka's short stories, at a page of *The Metamorphosis*: 'It was like a physical blow, the *absoluteness* of his prose.'

American literature rarely affected her the same way. There are few illuminating references to American writers. She's sniffy about Bellow ('has *not* ... produced a great body of work') and indifferent to Roth. Arthur Miller and Tennessee Williams don't get a mention. 'Weakness of American poetry – ' she writes, 'it's anti-intellectual.' There are two references to Lowell in Moser's book. None to Berryman or Plath. 'It is true,' writes David Rieff in the Preface to *Reborn*, 'that for her American literature was a suburb of the great literatures of Europe – above all German literature...' In 1967, reviewing *Against Interpretation*, Cyril Connolly noted that 'Miss Sontag has no use for the American novel...'

She never quite shook off the feeling of being the provincial from Arizona and California. 'My innocence makes me weep' she writes in her journal. Europe – which for her really meant Paris, Berlin, Venice (which she visited at least ten times) – was everything the schoolgirl from Tucson, Arizona longed to be. It meant being grown up, being intellectually and morally serious, in a way being American did not. Seriousness is a key word for Sontag.

The older she became, the more European. But her idea of 'Europe' changed, became darker, more elegiac. From the late 1970s and '80s, 'Europe' moved from Paris to central and east Europe. She had an important relationship with Joseph Brodsky. During the last thirty years of her life she wrote numerous essays on cultural figures from central and eastern Europe.[7]

A striking absence is her Jewishness. The daughter of Jack and Mildred Rosenblatt, the stepdaughter of Nathan Sontag, hasn't much to say about being Jewish or Jewish culture. 'Her Jewish origins were of scant interest to her,' writes Rieff in his memoir. It's the only reference to Jewishness in the whole book. There's barely a single reference to the Holocaust in Moser's 800-page volume. Look at the list of central and east European names. Just a few Jews among them.

A final puzzling absence which runs through Moser's biography: money. Moser chronicles the endless holidays. He lists a series of trips in the summer of 1966: London, Paris, Prague, back to London, back to Paris, Antibes, Venice ('first night "Gritti Palace [Hotel]", next three nights at the "Hotel Luna"'), back to Antibes, then Paris

and home to New York. Who pays for this? What does she live on as a freelance writer? Did *Partisan Review* and *Commentary* pay so well? Moser is fascinating about her relationships with patrons like Robert Silvers, her publisher Roger Straus and, above all, her long-term lover, the photographer Annie Leibovitz. Straus became her benefactor for years (and her occasional lover). He published all of her books, paid her advances for books she never wrote, often took care of her household bills, and contributed to her medical expenses. (He eventually hired her son David too, and kept him on the payroll for a decade.) Later on, Leibovitz paid for the mortgage, the maintenance, car services, a maid, a private chef, a studio, an office, assistants and vacations, and paid expenses for David. While they were together, Moser reports, she gave Sontag at least $8 million.

The financial costs of her medical treatment must have been enormous. Straus and Silvers helped raise money for the bills for her first two bouts of cancer, Leibovitz with the treatment for her final illness. Moser is damning about Sontag's extravagance and sense of entitlement. 'Her writings were peopled with divas,' he writes. It's clear he thinks she was the greatest diva of all.

Worst of all, though, are Moser's accounts of Sontag as a mother. In 1982, Sontag's thirty-year-old son David Rieff endured a number of major crises: cocaine addiction, job loss, romantic break-up, cancer scare and nervous breakdown. At that point, Moser writes, Sontag 'scampered off to Italy' with her new lover, the dancer and choreographer Lucinda Childs. 'We couldn't really believe she was getting on the plane', Kincaid told Moser. She and her husband Allen Shawn took David into their home for six months to recover. He made an impact writing about Bosnia. She flew into Sarajevo to direct *Godot* and hoovered up all the publicity.

There is much about the sadness of Sontag's life in Moser's biography, but little curiosity about depression as such. Relationships come to an end. Perhaps the most brutal ending was with Jasper Johns. There is a moment of crisis in 1971. 'How depressed I was', Sontag wrote. 'I wanted to die.' 'My life fell down.' 'I touch a central place, where I have never lived before... and I find, to my horror, that the center is mute.' This is what happens when she is saddest. Silence. No entries. 'Mute'.

And then the central question: what is the relationship between this tremendous energy, over forty years of prolific writing and lecturing, films, stories and novels – and the battle with depression? In 1979 she writes: 'I have an idea for a novel. A great idea.' She writes in the margin, '"*novel about melancholy*". It is, after all, my subject.' Later, she adds, 'Not for nothing was I born under the Sign of Saturn...' This obviously feeds into the title for her book of essays of the same name, published in 1980. In perhaps the best interview with Sontag, Kevin Jackson quotes her: 'I guess it's [loss, melancholy] my great theme. I would love to write a book called *The Anatomy of Melancholy*. It's the greatest title there is.'

It's one of the many books she never wrote. The journals are full of them. Which is the more telling: the energy that produced so many ideas for so many books? Or the obstacles that meant they were never written? There were so many brilliant essays but no single masterwork. In *Under the Sign of Saturn* she wonders about Benjamin's inability

---

7   Leni Riefenstahl (1975), Walter Benjamin (1978), Syberberg (1980), Canetti (1980), *Under the Sign of Saturn* (1980) was dedicated to Brodsky, Robert Walser (1982), Fassbinder (1983), Tsvetaeva (1983), Pina Bausch (a 1980s TV talk), 'Wagner's Fluids' (1987), 'The Idea of Europe' (1988), Danilo Kis (1995), Sebald (2000), Gombrowicz (2000), Zagajewski (2001), 'Waiting for Godot in Sarajevo' (1993), Brodsky (1997), Pasternak, Tsvetaeva and Rilke (2001), Victor Serge (2004), Leonid Tsypkin (published posthumously, 2005).

to achieve a major work. Ten pages later, she writes about Syberberg and the question of 'the Great Work'.

Pauline Kael dismissed her films. Kevin Costner's character in *Bull Durham* rubbished her novels. There is no academic industry dedicated to her work, in the way that there is about Foucault or Said. What, then, will endure? Her essays. In an interview in 1988 she said:

> there's this great tradition in my head, people like Emerson, Leopardi, Chamfort, Valery and Barthes – a wonderful tradition, with on the one hand the aphorism and on the other hand a certain kind of very tight, condensed essay writing: a field of intellectual force and writerly virtuosity that I feel an enormous affinity with. If I were to dare to describe my own aspiration it would be as someone who continues in that tradition, at whatever level of achievement. And it's a way of writing that breaks down the genres as we usually think of them: it's the tradition of the artist-thinker, the thinker as artist, that unites writers as disparate as Wilde, Nietzsche, Benjamin and Adorno.

What she had in common with all of these writers was her range of interests. She wrote on critics like Barthes and Benjamin, thinkers like Simone Weil, Camus and Cioran, filmmakers like Godard, Riefenstahl and Fassbinder, writers like Canetti, Sebald and Walser, dance, photography and art, politics from Cuba and Vietnam to Bosnia and Abu Ghraib. The old *Partisan Review* crowd wrote about literature and politics. She wrote about film, photography and pornography.

In a tribute written in 2005, Jonathan Rosenbaum wrote:

The last of the great New York intellectuals associated with *Partisan Review*, she was the only one in that crowd who understood and appreciated film in a wholly cosmopolitan manner, as a part of art and culture and thought – something that couldn't be said of Hannah Arendt, Saul Bellow, Irving Howe, Alfred Kazin, Mary McCarthy, Philip Rahv, Harold Rosenberg, Edmund Wilson, or any of the editors at the *New York Review of Books*.

Then there is her most distinctive gift as a critic: her originality. Her best-known work was associated with opening up new subjects: 'camp', 'the pornographic imagination', photography, illness, torture. And there was the originality of the questions she asked: What are fascist aesthetics? Why is Nazism erotic? Why are we fascinated by suffering bodies? Why are TB and cancer the great metaphorical illnesses? How did Kafka understand China – from Prague – in 1918-1919? Why are Jews and homosexuals the outstanding creative minorities in contemporary urban culture? Like her contemporaries, John Berger and George Steiner, she was a new kind of cultural critic. Perhaps this was what drew her to Walter Benjamin and Roland Barthes. They wanted to write about a new kind of culture, beyond the library.

In 2005 Susan Sontag was buried in Montparnasse Cemetery in Paris. It was the perfect choice, the most literary of cemeteries. Near de Beauvoir, one hundred metres from Beckett, two hundred from Cioran. But there's another reason why it was the perfect choice. Paris was where Sontag was reborn almost fifty years before. It's where she found her voice as one of the great essayists of her time.

Odyssey Response

Vahni Capildeo

I. Words, take wing
Words, take wing, fly commonly among all people
who have power of health and employment over us;
go like the sparrows rife on summer streets of a holy
island; unlearn any fear; flitting, bring to mind
light, and how quickly light fades; bring to mind life,
comfort in houses, fragile as windows onto space.
Words, take wing, as if lawyers were angels, as if death
were a paper doll in a set of identical
paper dolls, an infinite set of paper doll kings
of terror, cancelled by a gentle fiery sword.
Sometimes, words, you launch in many lovely languages; yet,
before you begin to fly, you are misrecognized,
like an owl entering a superstitious person's
open-plan room being beaten to death, Athena's
wise bird struck down, bloody feathers everywhere,

a soft body a futile piñata
releasing clouds. Could you gather up a faith
in strangers, in the absence of a god of strangers?
Does any homeless person gleam like a god in disguise?
Disgust rules. Do without. Doing without big symbols.
Zeus! Eagles may acquire cruel associations.
Words, take wing, fly commonly among all people
who share vulnerability on a trembling earth;
who drink, or hope to drink, sweetly, cool water.

II. HERO?

Tell me how to simplify a song. Tell me about
identity; fidelity. Solve the problem of a face.
Tell me about a state governed by emotion – would you move?
Choose to move? If they force you into moving?
If you cannot afford to, cannot afford not to –
Make a song about one person. Who can cope.
        Is it a hero you want? Why not say so?
I am suspicious of heroes. How do they survive?
I know a mother who scattered her children
on the way out of war, and has not gone back to look.
What if the hero shining like a falcon arrives
having traded their body for life, trailing killings
and transactional sex? Is the hero empowered
to treat their spouse to raw cuts of trauma, treat them worse
and better than anyone else? Help can be a trap.
Home, a mating of traps. Who do you want at your back?
Enough. I am privileged to have civil conversations
in a corrected city, commemorate the correct dead.
        How changeable is a hero, like modern rainfall patterns.
How fearful is a hero, patched like an archaic sail.
How lifted up is a hero, like the great-grandchild
of immigrants, hurting his parents, hoping his child is kind.
Witness those ghosts who, after a natural disaster, don't know
they're dead; poor, wet ghosts, trying to board real taxis home.

III. THE SEA

Hooves, chevrons, arrowheads, champion ski racers, nothing, no,
nothing runs so swiftly, nothing seems to run so, so
swiftly as cool water pours back in, making
an island of a piece of land once, sometimes, no more
than another part of the shore, a tidal island.
Nothing runs so swiftly. Did you think I was singing
about death? Should we give death preferential treatment?
Should we be women singing to death? You saw. You know.
The sea is a cover for bones, how busyness covers news.
New bodies are laid every day in the innocence
of the sea. New burdens explode every day
in the innocence of the air. How many
of my family dropped like shining falcons
in the duress of a forced migration, ivorying
into the sunken halls of the only Atlantis
really worthy of the name? The sea is a cover.
There is a law of the sea – No. The sea is lawless. –
There is a modern law of the sea. The conference
proceeded for nine years. – No. It is a convention
of the toothless, for the toothless, by the toothless. The sea needs
teeth. – How can there be freedom of the sea without protection? –
How can you be territorial about the sea?
Most of the civilized – America never agreed. Never –

IV. COMPANION

I tremble to think of meeting you. How did we meet
on this trembling earth?
A blizzard blew up. We sat
on a stone, a few paces from the farmhouse.
We could not see, or move, to go to them. They could not
come to us. We could not discern the tide, rising towards us.
     How did we meet?
     He had turned his back on you. I loved
the poetry of your anger. I wanted the poetry
of your anger on my small island. Transported. Cherished.
Forget any other kind of kiss.
     I tremble to think of not meeting you. You could be
better off. Light was fading quickly. You saw. You knew
I was unsafe, waiting, in my full-passported femaleness
in the cruel associations of a village
of privileged abandonment. You sat on the bench,
reached beyond death into Persia at your back,
unrolled for me a mat of pure imagination,
placed for us both a vase of pure imagination.
Your metamorphosis was from refugee to host.
In the street, you gathered guest-right, offered me
hospitality where had been others' hostility, till
my neglectful, official friend arrived. We thrived, like two birds
in an embroidery orchard of pomegranates, oranges,
and weeping pears: like impossibilities of climate
redemption.
     They spin epic words to say none of this is home.

V. HADES SOCIAL

Be thankful for the friends in a blue and white country
who invite you to meet their dead. Together, in a small group,
crossing the clean-smelling river pierced by mossy rocks,
enter among tombs like garden sheds, houses;
graves with lost names, granite pitted by acid rainfall patterns.
Rub flowerless hands over lost names. – Try not to bring
anyone home with you, someone invisible says
in your memory, sharpening into many voices,
women singing to death.
     What is this place? How did you get here?
You know. Graveyards are unclean. The only way to go
is by fire open to the sky, on fragrant woods,
white camphor tucked under your tongue, releasing spirit
from the ragged body to the innocence of air.
– I cannot be burnt, I cannot burn as I need to
burn, among these new friends, these kind friends, thinks the stranger.
Be glad to meet the new kind dead your friends have buried. You saw.
Next time bring flowers. – But I am sad for my future,
in a country where my funeral customs are illegal.
Whose problem is a soul? Identity? Fidelity? Death
is a thief in a stationery shop. He strolls out.
The shopkeeper, a poor man, runs after, shouting. – I saw you!
Give that back! – Give back what? Death says, strolling out.
Hermes is a tram attendant who holds your coffee,
helping you find the coin you dropped; it rolls underfoot.

VI. THE FACES OF ODYSSEUS

When the trembling earth dips away from our common ancestor,
a wife living as a widow may look at the streaks and stripes
of another seaside sunset, beauty in isolation,
and tremble like the earth at the men lined up
to land on her like shining falcons, quickly, but not lightly.
If an old person perseveres in life, yet needing your care,

do not harass or tease them as Odysseus did,
tricking his father into hardworking tears, washing his brain
with real grief and reactive gladness.
You know, you see Christ in the face of a wounded enemy,
if you listen to the now-celebrated poets weeping.
What if you hear the song of yourself simplified on the news?
What if your song is impermissible as the blacked-out news?
Odysseus, I see you. I know I thought I might
dislike you. You were so hot. You planned it: standing naked, hot,
in the doorway, drawing the long bow no-one else could.
Standing where Penelope could see the slaughter of fine men
her hero would commit, war for an indoor Helen.
I see you in the face of the vagrant thoughtfully
washing his clothes at the standpipe in the Savannah
under the trees with no-one to care. No-one, Odysseus.
One man's soldier is another man's beggar, Odysseus.
He lives without love or teasing, sweet talk or complication.
One woman's king is another woman's case, Odysseus.

VII. Zeus, god of strangers
Stranger, how are you cast away, cast upon your own
resources, cast on wildly different styles of hosting?
What if your angry host feeds you up to go to war?
What if the gifts lavished on you lay expectations on you
to go away, make a success of yourself, and don't come back?
What if you are blown back, empty-handed? You would be
right to hide your name. Yes? You are a king at home. No?
Slaughter and laughter cross your threshold
in your absence. Slaughter and laughter at a distance
shadow and echo you, no matter how you set off,
or your clean presentation, now, among the élite. Yes? No?
Where are you? Islands aren't always islands. All maps are pop-up.
Volcanos yawn, spatter out something the sea covers over.
Rivers rise, or silt up. Clumps form, or dissolve, barely the size
for two blue-coated Norsemen to duel on.
Islands are provisional. World; whirl. The sea covers over.
The Queen of the Dead lifts, in her lily hand
with its violet nails, a head of snakehair.
Do not go too deep. That way paralysis. You want action,
like tired people do. Stranger, you are cast like in a dream
of being on stage, unprepared. Is it right to invent lines?
Traveller in body, buffeted about as a guest, Zeus
loves us. Spirit Traveller, revive as a good host. By Zeus,
Time Traveller, if you see Columbus, shoot on sight.

VIII. That's epic
There is a city beneath the city beneath the city
beneath the floodplain. Forget about it. A city
is at the back of the city at the back of the city.
Ignore it. Ignore the scripts in which mathematics
and astronomy were first written. Ignore the scripts
incised in rock, the scripts inscribed in landscape.
O Muse, make the poet move on. Memory is no good
to triumphant civilizations.
O Muse, your poet is blind, saying life has a sheen.
O Muse, your poet's a hostage, saying land has a meaning.
Nobody likes a try-hard, a lacemaker working
with a vascular surgeon to join delicate gaps.
Put memory in the service of intention
to keep the story shining, like tears shed over onionskin,
or the cheering faces of the well-fed family watching
screensful of migrants plummeting or washed up
at a border, from a wall. The camera admires
guards, themselves descended from migrants.
The shining chorus of weaponry,
made manifest by taxes, drops death
on more children shining and their many lovely languages
as if they were done for from the get-go, like paper brochures
in a digital age. Forget about it.
Keep going. A story has the tricks of appetite.

Poems in English

MARK DOW

Cough

Mami, mamá,
quiero irme a
casa pero
¿cuándo? Now.
Right now. Mamá,
en la escuela
aprendí *discuss*.
Discuss es hablar.
Eso aprendi-
mos: *discuss*.
Mami, tengo
tos. Quiero
ir right now.

Tuna

'na empanada,
qué rica. Sí, ¿no?
Ya no hay. You
hungry? Hay tuna.
Okay, dame una.

Cricket

English I learn listening
to cricket com*men*tary,
Australian com*men*-
tary. Nineteen eighty-
two to nineteen ninety-
five just listen to
Australian cricket com-
*men*tary. Usually that
time is radio, not TV,
just usually always watch
the radio. Always they
had very nice com*men*-
tary, Australian com*men*-
tary. They speak English
so I always understand
English now. Cricket is
big entertainment now.
It first name is
gentlemen game.
Cricket is gentlemen
game, not bad-people
game. First the name
is crick. Just crick.
Then it improve and later
the name is called cricket.
In school we have English
lessons but always I run
away from lessons. That's
why I'm never learn English.
Just run away and only play
cricket. My father he is
always angry. He always
love the hockey, never
cricket, always tell me
why do I love the cricket.
Why you love so much
the cricket? Maybe that
is the reason why
I always run to play.

New Orleans

Ching chong ching chong ching. Wait, what?
I think that how you think it sound,
like I say *ching chong ching chong ching*,
you think that how the Chinese sound.
Aren't you Vietnamese? I thought
you were from Vietnam. Yes, we
from Vietnam but customer
they always think we are Chinese.
They say that how the talk it sound.

South Florida

The Haitian they speak mess-up French. Mess-up.
House they say *lakay la*, but French we say *maison*.
I don't see nothing to do with French. Or *children* in
French is *les enfants*, in Creole is *timoun.* They have
nothing to do. They are very far. It is mess-up French
'cause their French it is not really real. Too many stuff
is missing. I don't see nothing to do with French. I un-
derstand it but to talk to them it's very hard. Me, I have
three language. I'm French but Arabic from Morocco
and I understand English. You have to slow down. Just
talk like that? No way. Slow down. Return the car, where's
the terminal, where where where, there there there, so fast,
no way. Sometimes people understand me. I live in Pompano
two years, work here, maybe some Americans don't want me.
When I see their face their faces say, especially I'm also Arab,
Morocco, I tell by the face, even they don't say nothing I
can tell. I don't mind. Some people only. Not all. Oh well.

Clerk

You ride your horse, can't eat your horse.
The way they call rich people they say
he have 500 horses. 500 horses mean
he is rich person, eat and ride, Kazaks
eat horse, ride horse, why not, because
so many of them they can both. You eat
lamb or beef or horse kebab. You just try.
Kazaks are nomad. My grandparents nomad.
That's why for us the horse mean everything.
You just try this one adapter charger you
put inside cigarette lighter for USB port
for phone and AC power too. USB mean
universal serial bus where you connect to port.
But not a bus like bus you ride somewhere.
It stand for *omnibus.* Mean everything.

James Atlas

the Shadow and the Poet

TONY ROBERTS

LITERARY BIOGRAPHY IS, like criticism, one of the ugly sisters of poetry – and not simply because its sales are better. Behind all the carping – the 'loud chorus of negativity', as James Atlas described it – is the feeling that the written life is not only irrelevant to the art but can marginalize, substitute for, or even extinguish it.

On the other hand one could argue that ephemerality is more the result of changing attitudes and fashions in society. Atlas found that out with his first biography, of the poet Delmore Schwartz, whose reputation is now 'sadly diminished', as John Ashbery observed in 2016.

While not as immersive as Robert Caro, who went to live with Lyndon Johnson's neighbours in an early stage of his research, or as intense as Richard Holmes, for whom biography is 'a kind of pursuit', Atlas was never-theless highly skilled, imaginative, and indefatigable in his research ('a biographer more scrupulous than Atlas is hard to imagine', according to 'The New York Times'). In contrast to Holmes, whom he greatly admired, he acknowledged in an interview, 'I'm a distinctly anti-ro-mantic biographer: brooding, fatalistic, cynical – though not entirely unsympathetic to our human plight'.

Born in Evanston, Illinois, in 1949, Atlas studied at Harvard and Oxford as a Rhodes Scholar, where the influ-ence of his tutor Richard Ellmann helped turn him from poetry to biography. In the course of his career he con-tributed to 'The New Yorker', 'The New York Times Mag-azine', 'The New York Review of Books' and other influential magazines, became an editor, novelist and publisher (of Atlas Books) and founded the biographical series 'Penguin Lives' and later 'Eminent Lives'. He was also the author of two biographies: the stunning (and stunned) *Delmore Schwartz: The Life of an American Poet* (1977) and, in 2000, *Bellow: A Biography.* (In a grim irony, Atlas was eventually diagnosed with bipolarity. He recognised he had been closer to Schwartz than he had known forty years before, when writing the book.) Before his death in September 2019, Atlas's ruminations on his life with the genre appeared as *The Shadow in the Garden: A Biogra-pher's Tale*.

Two early pieces he published in 'PN Review' illustrate his preparation. The substantial essay 'Literary Biography' is both revealing of Atlas's values as a biographer as well as being an edu-cation in the mainsprings of twentieth century biography.

He begins with the felt need of other practi-tioners to venture into theoretical justification of their genre, 'to vindicate themselves not only before the tribunal of the living, but also before their vanquished subjects, whose recriminations are no less effective for being mute'. He turns to a consideration of Leon Edel's method, to which Atlas subscribes. In Edel's conception, the writer's role is to explore the subjective as well as the dramatic in a life, while scrupulously avoiding remaking the subject in his image.

This leads to discussion of the complexity brought to biography by the turn to Freudian interpretation, including the need to acknowledge not impersonality but identification. Moving beyond Victorian concealment and innuendo, the biographer is now seen 'interposed, in a version of relativity, between his subject and the reality of his subject's life, which appears before us refracted through the lens of the biographer's own temperament'.

After considering 'that intuitive chronicler of sensibility, Lytton Strachey', most comprehensive in his exploration of the non-dramatic details of a life, Atlas explores in some detail the work of three classic biographers: George Painter (Proust), Edel (Henry James) and Ellmann (James Joyce). These have contributed to 'the peculiarly modern deification of personality', addressing themselves in one way or another to 'the attempt to render consciousness as an event no less important than those external incidents that formerly made up the substance of biography'. All are magnificent in their work and admiring of their subjects, according to Atlas, though Painter ('the most remarkable of modern literary biographies') is admittedly reactionary, Edel ('sprawling, eloquent work') evasive and Ellmann ('astonishing and generous') is at times condescending.

In a *Poetry Nation* (later *PN Review*) review from 1975 of *Pity the Monsters: The Political Vision of Robert Lowell* we find Atlas applauding good critical practice: 'Alan Williamson, while establishing necessary connections between Lowell's poems and what is known of his personal life, does so only to plot the nature and origins of those conflicts which provide a unified motif in the span of Lowell's work.' Implicit in the comment is his belief that the task of the biographer should encompass this.

The front cover photo on my 1978 paperback copy of *Delmore Schwartz* (reproduced again on *The Shadow in the Garden*) boasts the perfect metaphor for biography. It is the celebrated 1938 Vogue portrait of Schwartz seen in the mirror, as if it were over the shoulder of his shadowed biographer. In terms of its subject, it has the appropriately Freudian association of narcissism and Wildean self-destructiveness. The subtitle prioritizes the poetry, though Schwartz was equally known for his stories and admired for his essays. There was a time in the forties though when he reigned as the most anthologized of American poets, so much so that he could fantasise posterity would deploy the term 'Delmorean'. It has not.

Delmore Schwartz was born in Brooklyn to Romanian Jewish parents on December 8, 1913. His father made a great deal of money before dying young and Schwartz found his relationship with his demanding mother something of a life-long trial. He was educated variously at Columbia, Wisconsin and New York universities, spending time also at Harvard, where he returned to teach. Success came with the appearance of the 1937 short story, 'In Dreams Begin Responsibilities', in the newly relaunched 'Partisan Review'. It became the title of his book of poetry and prose which garnered the most prestigious praise (from Pound, Eliot, Williams, Tate and others). Later collections fared less well, especially commercially, though the short stories *The World is a Wedding*

(1948) was a critical success and *Summer Knowledge: New and Selected Poems* (1959), was awarded the Bollingen Prize.

Schwartz taught at a number of universities and worked as poetry editor at 'Partisan Review' and 'New Republic'. Yet the surface glamour of this summary conceals the self-destructiveness of the man. His energies dissipated in alcohol and narcotics; his two marriages failed; his precarious mental health undermined his relationships and, toward the end, his work. He alienated his many friends, became severely paranoid and litigious and died of a heart attack at the Columbia Hotel near Times Square in July 1966.

As we learn from *The Shadow in the Garden*, the biography had its origins in a chance barroom conversation between the son of Schwartz's friend, Dwight Macdonald, and the owner of a removal company which held the papers of the recently deceased poet. He had died unnoticed. Atlas was offered a contract at the age of twenty-five to write the life. No-one would ever scrutinise Schwartz more exhaustively than James Atlas – except the man himself.

His life might have absorbed future generations – a life with such a dramatically downward spiral and one so well told – yet ironically it is the work which marginalized it. Schwartz seems too set in his generation and, as Atlas put it in an article about the New York intellectuals (the 'Partisan Review' crowd): 'the passions that animated the 30's and 40's are history.' He is too solely preoccupied with Jewish experience ('the Jew in America', Eileen Simpson styled his theme in *Poets in their Youth*, her classic memoir of marriage to Schwartz's friend, John Berryman). The stories fail to transcend the experience of that Jewish generational bind: the ambitions of immigrant parents versus those of their (literary) children. At the same time – ever the Freudian – Schwartz's obsessive exploration of himself in his poetry, while bordering on the tragic, ultimately slackens and tires.

Atlas's biography, however, still reads as vividly as it did on its first appearance. He had detected behind Ellmann's Joyce the biographer himself. It was a voice like that, 'scholarly but not academic', that he aspired to. He had learnt the lesson, 'If you trust the writer's voice, you'll trust the writer's facts'. From a position close to omniscience, Atlas's own voice avoids condescension or a censorious tone, exhibiting discretion in what might easily have offered itself as a subject for sensationalism.

He presents Schwartz as brilliant student of T. S. Eliot, whose Modernist detachment he adopted; a fine poet and teacher who focused on Literature as appreciation; a first class essayist-critic of the American scene (Hemingway, Tate, Faulkner); and an admirer of Blackmur, Tate and Wilson. He is also depicted as arrogant, obsessed with his Jewishness, impractical, improvident, alienated, dependent on women whom he abused emotionally, capable of self-hatred and remorse as well as great friendships. ('I remember his electrical insight as the young man, / his wit & passion, gift, the whole young man / alive with surplus love', wrote John Berryman in 'Dream Song 155'.)

Atlas rockets through his narrative giving the drama in the life, while adding a little permissible colouring at times: 'In the fall of 1936, Delmore returned to Harvard in the midst of its tercentenary celebration. More cynical than reverent, he listened to the pompous speeches, observed the grandiose parades festooned with crimson VERITAS banners and noted the celebrities in attendance.'

With the bonus of the journals, he is able to convey something of his subject's mental turmoil: 'Delmore had never regarded his birthdays with equanimity, but this December 8 was more ominous than ever, for he was turning thirty "and deceived by inspiration and losing hope & hope's lies." Writing to Berryman that morning he tried to be light-hearted.'

Atlas's characterisation of the poet's style is pithy: 'Delmore's amazing rhetoric, the orotund, passionate expression of grief and rage recited in varied pentameters, owed as much to what he thought to be the high style of nineteenth-century French poetry as it did to his American elders.' He refers to the characteristic voice as 'sonorous, faintly archaic', producing 'uneven blank verse' and to a 'Byronic element in his character, combined with the subtle tonalities of a wry Jewish ironist'.

Atlas also reveals a sound understanding of the context of Schwartz's work, which he expresses in terms of American Modernism and the complex influence of Pound and Eliot, while observing that William Carlos Williams 'was the only poet who carried on the work of Modernism at home'. He also deals with the unsavoury issue of 'the antipathy to Jews that persisted in the English Departments of Ivy League universities well into the forties'. (We might note here Richard J. Evans' recent comment in a 'Times Literary Supplement' review about 'the ingrained antisemitism of many of the [Oxford] dons' a little earlier in the century.)

An entertaining feature of the biography is Atlas's use of humorous anecdotes. On one occasion Schwartz, the young student, comes to his professor's rescue with 'salt' when the philosopher cannot finish the expression 'take with a pinch of...'. The thankful professor, Alfred North Whitehead, breathes a sigh of relief: 'Yes, yes, I knew I was something mineral!' On another occasion there is an amusing story about Schwartz beginning to enlighten a member of the Hartford Insurance Company about Wallace Stevens's poetic genius, when interrupted by his friend's observation that the old man was a lousy insurance lawyer and would have been fired long before if he had not been a great poet.

Behind Atlas's conception of biography was his belief in the literary tradition. In his contribution to the 'great books' argument in 1990, with *Battle of the Books: The Curriculum Debate in America*, he took a stand in favour of the canon as a defence 'of the claims of society' above those of the individual in the belief – as one of his interviewees expressed it – that the struggle over canonical status was 'a struggle among contending factions for the right to be represented in the picture America draws of itself '. Although his ideas remained conservative (and remain contentious) his position clearly illustrated a commitment to traditional notions of Literature and criticism widely adhered to in our generation.

According to a 'New York Times' blog interview, the title of Atlas's memoir, *The Shadow in the Garden*, comes from Bellow and its method from Janet Malcolm, whose biographical explorations subvert biography itself.

Although a personal memoir of a life in the business, the reader finds reference to a wide number of biographers (including Boswell, Ellmann, Edel, Holmes, Marchand, Strachey), as well as critics (Macdonald, Wilson, Kazin, Rahv, Allan Bloom, Malcolm), writers and academics (Joyce, Isaac Rosenfeld, Edward Shils) and, of course, his own biographical subjects, Schwartz and Bellow.

Considering the purpose of biography as a genre, Atlas offers the following, surely uncontentious, explanation: 'Primarily, I would say, to show what other factors – besides genius – contributed to the making of the writer's life, the genesis of his books, the social and literary influences that formed them.' Where he becomes more personal is in recognizing the impulse that set him off on his career: 'I was beginning to sense that the lives of poets interested me even more than the poetry. I could recite Robert Lowell's 'Skunk Hour' in its entirety... but I was also curious about the car crash that nearly killed his first wife, Jean Stafford, while he was driving. I thrilled to the onomato-poetic mutterings of Eliot reading "The Waste Land" on the Caedmon album I owned, but I still wanted to know why he had locked away *his* first wife, Vivienne Haigh-Wood, in a mental institution. Art and life didn't just coexist: they enriched each other.' The higher gossip?

In preparation he read countless biographies, focusing on how they worked 'with the absorption of a car mechanic' as he puts it in the book. After Schwartz he made a living partly by reviewing biographies, preparing for his subjects by 'speed-reading their books and previous biographies in marathon sessions at the New York Public Library; after a week or so of late nights, I usually knew enough to write a passably well-informed review'.

He learnt also that some sort of empathy with his subject was a prerequisite for the necessary years of work involved. It was largely for reasons of incompatibility that Atlas returned an advance to write on the famous WASP and waspish Edmund Wilson (a work later done excellently by Lewis M. Dabney – despite Atlas's dismissal of it and the Jeffrey Meyers biography as 'adequate'). This may have been an even shrewder move than he knew, since he admits to not being able to finish Wilson's magnum opus, *Patriotic Gone* (an outstanding work and a masterpiece of atmosphere – except that it omits African American experience). *The Shadow in the Garden* ends with Atlas worrying over the future of books and biography and about whether to dump the 'detritus' of his last research.

While literary biography *is* at best a 'shadow', even a quasi-fiction, it does allow the reader behind the scenes and into the company of not one but two writers. It is unlikely that James Atlas ever seriously regretted being one of them: 'I had devoted my life to an art whose assumptions couldn't be tested,' he wrote. 'Still, its rewards could be great – the challenge of reconstructing someone else's world; the opportunity to educate yourself; the serendipitous encounters and unlikely finds. I found this invigorating.' The evidence is in the books.

Venice, Florida and other poems

A N G E   M L I N K O

Venice, Florida

The clouds went on each afternoon –
bodybuilding to a rippling mass,
flat-topped, or with bedhead;
from a puffball, picayune,
they did something to the grass
fluorescing on the watershed.

It rained so hard all summer long,
every field was canalized
by overflow, or turned into lagoon.
The fountain jets burped a song
of bullfrogs poolside, bullseyed,
prelude to a honeymoon.

Electricity's appendages, like
butterfly filaments, alighted on things,
charging the soil with nitrogen,
so you'd run, as though Nike
grabbed your ankles by their wings,
and you were an Olympian.

On one of these afternoons,
you met your tennis coach,
storms needling the atmosphere,
clouds like hydroponic blooms,
roots whitening on approach.
You should have shown more fear,

hitting balls that greenly blazed
in the hyacinthine climate;
like statuary, your torso flexed
on tiptoe, your arm upraised
to execute a serve, until the wet
match fizzled out. (There's a text

that warns boys of hubris!)
Then things would clear.
A dragonfly would gondolier
through the misted air and seem
to offer a golden balance beam
to the showboating iris.

A calmness floods the aftermath.
This is the secret of summer eves,
when ultramarine bands the earth,
twin of the blue hour in the north.
Not snow fields, but grass and leaves
dusk milks blue for all they're worth.

The Elegance Of Pelicans

Along the fishing pier that dashes into the Gulf at Naples
on legs like a stop motion photograph of a runner
multiplied at speed, lace-making waves swishing at his ankles,
three pelicans lunged at a blowfish that managed to
unhook itself from a lure, and adding feat to feat,
bewildered the ravenous birds by puffing itself up

so that the pelican that caught it startled; another took it up,
only to drop it instantly, and with half of Naples
looking on, cheering, the third gave it a try, and met defeat.
As they disported, thwarted, the blowfish like a rubber
ball allowed itself to be passed and dribbled from one to
another until, finagling its own interception at the ankles

of its opponents, shrank, and sank among the barnacles.
This story, from the correspondence of Elizabeth Bishop,
is rather like the incident related in *Mozart's Journey to
Prague,* about two boating parties in the Bay of Naples.
Only one of them was stocked with girls. A rudder
pointed right at them, and a basket at their feet

stocked with oranges suggested a defense. Playfully, fête
galante-style, the girls pelted the boys' ankles
with flying oranges, and athwart a slender rider
of the waves pitching, yawing, and rearing up,
each pulled off a volley for the passeggiata of Naples,
with great finesse and mirth, hand to

hand across the gunwales. There was a band, too,
playing saltarelli and canzones against the buffet
of oranges, the flashing azure of the Bay of Naples,
which lifted the lace hems at the girls' ankles
as it rocked them. When the boys climbed up
into their boat, one took the prettiest, and rid her

of her cad. (A sail unfurled, depicting Cupid.) A reader,
accounting for the change in sensibility between two
centuries, might still conclude they don't add up.
But between the feat of the blowfish and the feat
of the suitors on the wavelets, a chime as of anklets
is my cue to keep skimming pages for more Naples.

Like an underground runner of some wild fruit, Naples
creeps up to your feet, bursting through the soil
to clap you by the ankles, only to start flowering!

Egrets, Herons, Cranes, Ibises...

We don't have much time; what there is of it
seems slower because we're engulfed by sun
on a wide flat prairie whose grassy palette
conceals so much in its variegation

that our gaze takes a long while to travel
across the broad swathe at our feet.
Were we to examine it on a swivel,
a circle would take an hour to complete –

just as the three-mile loop does. Birders
carrying cameras come from all over
to see the species transcend borders
for an exotic grub to discover,

or pond to plunder, fitted at birth
(as we are not) with a tiny magnet
to help align them with the earth,
the latitute-longitude dragnet

drawn out on our grade school maps –
or else they know to navigate by stars
on their cross-continental trips,
as attentive to pattern as to particulars.

At any rate, we come for the waterfowl,
mostly, who come for this water park,
hanging out to dry without a towel
or taking to the sky to make no mark.

Zero swans, French hens, turtledoves
or partridges here, and mockingbirds
– spurning the afflatus of true loves! –
prefer places with more, not fewer, words.

When all falls away to sigh and murmur,
a lone anhinga commands a post:
in tux colors, he's conductor,
and gestures to the heavenly host,

shoulders risen, wings extended.
Really, there's something not funny at all
– just too human – in the unbefriended
sounds that issue from the caterwaul:

a bleat, a bleep, a honk; a syrinx fissile,
deviated, its signal lapsed into wind ...
yet each bird (to our eyes so replete a vessel!)
strains to hear another of its kind.

Three Poems

Leeanne Quinn

Smoke

Winter fills my lungs with smoke,
I breathe in the new year
in this old house. Winter of locked doors,

empty rooms, winter of ill winds,
thrashing rains. Winter,
was I always this afraid?

Smoke billows from the bonnet,
I think 'house' not 'car.'
I think beautiful bonfire. I think

your blood into flames, your charts
into char. I think with your precision.
O how we both know precisely

more than the other now – you,
how to go, me, how to go without.
Yet, here you are

asking from across another winter's
divide – *are you okay?*
Answer first and I swear...

Smoke billows into the black sky,
our lives for kindling, ash
will mark our loss in the morning.

Not at All Like the Sea

'The sea – is here, and – not here.' — Marina Tsvetaeva

And what kind of silence is the silence
of seeing the sea behind glass as white
waves crash without sound, without.

The ridge of the waves is a ridge of ice
covering the ridge of a mountain,
the waves are tankers, or roads

revealed by tankers. Is that the sea?
*That's not the sea at all, not at all
like the sea.* And, of course, how could it be?

The sea holds you horizontal,
what can I do with that? Waves
cannot be walked, the sea

can only bring me under,
like love. I want to be high
in the blue mountain,

I want to be the mountain, high
in the blue, above this soft,
above this silent sea.

September

Wasps, then rain. Below, streets clear
to a silent siren. Some citizens scatter,
others stand looking upwards.

Wasps nestle into the neck
of abandoned sugar canisters, the wood
of balconies sways.

In parks the remnants of summer
still – dug-up earth, a brittle mound
of clay, some small animal's refuge.

The leaves here are beginning to fall.
Sun bleached, they swirl like shadows
in the *Föhn*, like shadows adjusting.

Hart Crane 'from this side'

Edgell Rickword and *The Calendar of Modern Letters*

FRANCESCA A. BRATTON

BEFORE THE BORISWOOD EDITION of his *Complete Poems* was published in London in 1938, Hart Crane's reputation in the UK rested on, as F.R. Leavis put it in his review of the volume in *Scrutiny*, 'the odds and ends of him one came on in American periodicals, together with the kind of claims made for him by the critics'. It was 'at last possible for the reader on this side of the Atlantic to come to a conclusion about the legend of Hart Crane'. While it is true that it would have been easier to lay hands on essays and reminiscences of Crane written by Allen Tate or Malcolm Cowley in a UK bookshop, Leavis seems to have missed or forgotten Crane's appearances in London-based magazines. Crane's poetry was published in both T.S. Eliot's *The Criterion* (1922–39) and Edgell Rickword's *Calendar of Modern Letters* (1925–1927), whose 'Scrutinies' feature gave its name to Leavis' own journal.

Edgell Rickword joined the Artists Rifles in 1916, serving with the Royal Berkshire Regiment as an officer. Following the Armistice, he was awarded the Military Cross and was invalided out of the army. Rickword's first collection of poems, *Behind the Eyes*, was published in 1921, followed by *Invocation to Angels* (1928) and *Twittingpan and Some Others* (1931), with his *Collected Poems* appearing in 1947. Rickword founded and edited the influential *Calendar of Modern Letters* with Douglas Garman and Bertram Higgins, receiving financial backing from publisher Ernest Wishart. He went on to work as an associate editor at the *Left Review* from 1934-1938.

Compared to *The Criterion*, Rickword's magazine was far more sympathetic to Crane's poetry, and to U.S. poets more generally. Crane was keen to receive Eliot's seal of approval though, and read Eliot's rejection letters with an amusing, if unwarranted optimism: after 'To Brooklyn Bridge' was politely returned, he told Harry and Caresse Crosby of the Parisian Black Sun Press that Eliot 'urges me to contribute' to a future issue. Although Eliot wrote to Crane's mother Grace after his death in 1932, telling her that 'much of his work I admired very much. There are very few living poets in America of equal interest to me', he returned all but one of Crane's five submissions. 'The Tunnel', the section of *The Bridge* in which Crane is most engaged with Eliot, was the only poem accepted for publication in *The Criterion*.

Among the journals active within the London literary scene in the late 1920s, *The Calendar* and *The Criterion* stand out for their engagement with modernist literature – though the two magazines printed different constellations of American writers. As Jason Harding has noted, 'Eliot declined submissions from William Carlos Williams, Gertrude Stein, John Crowe Ransom, Allen Tate, Laura Riding, R. P. Blackmur and F. Scott Fitzgerald' – many of whom appeared in *The Calendar*. Rickword, meanwhile, regularly reviewed U.S. poetry for the *TLS*, and was likely the anonymous reviewer of Crane's first collection, *White Buildings*. Other publications, such as *The London Mercury*, were hostile to the kind of writing Rickword and his associate editors wanted to publish: 'They wrote things like "You can't get blood out of a Stein"', as Rickword later told Michael Schmidt and Alan Young in an interview in *Poetry Nation*. Rickword described *The Calendar* as 'sort of a discontented club, discontented with all the established novelists and literary cliques' – including that gathered around *The Criterion*. The 'anti-modernist' and 'anti-American' stance of other U.K. journals, he added, was crucial to *The Calendar*'s conception of the 'sluggishness' of the British literary scene. *The Calendar* tackled this 'sluggishness' in their 'Scrutinies' column, in which the editors established their own 'standards of criticism'. The aspiration was in part, as Rickword's biographer Charles Hobday has put it, to pierce the 'inflated reputations' of 'their elders...a guilty generation that had sent them to war'.

Crane's 'Three Songs from *The Bridge*', published in the final number of *The Calendar* in 1927, marked his second appearance in the magazine. The previous year, Rickword had accepted and published three of Crane's poems: 'At Melville's Tomb', 'Praise for an Urn' and 'Passage'. Each show Crane's increasing interest in associative, complex metaphor, and had been hard to place in U.S. journals. 'At Melville's Tomb' was famously the source of Harriet Monroe's consternation over Crane's 'confused... champion mixed metaphors', prompting his defence published alongside the poem in *Poetry*, in which Crane first publicly outlined his 'logic of metaphor'.

Crane deemed Rickword's magazine 'a very decent quarterly', and it is likely he was introduced to *The Calendar* by Laura Riding. Rickword and Crane met in London in 1927 during Crane's brief trip to the city. Ever in need of 'a little change for the purse', part of his interest in the journal was, no doubt, their generous rates of pay, which Rickword believed would help the journal secure the best contributors. Rickword was intrigued by Crane's submissions and requested a copy of *White Buildings*, published by Boni & Liveright in 1926. His interest in Crane's first collection was sincere, and Rickword made a serious attempt to secure the publication of *White Buildings* with *The Calendar*'s publisher, Wishart & Company, Ernest Wishart's experimental publishing house (which later became Lawrence & Wishart, publishing materials for the Communist Party of Great Britain).

Rickword wrote to Boni & Liveright in New York City, enquiring how much a print run of 350 copies would cost. 'Though the market for poetry, and particularly for such "difficult" poetry as Hart Crane's is small, we are anxious to issue that book in this country, if there is any prospect of our being able to recover a reasonable proportion of the cost of doing so.' Both publishers deemed the enterprise too costly, and Crane's poetry was not available in volume form in the U.K. until the Boriswood edition.

There are glimpsed-at affinities between the different poetic sensibilities of Crane and Rickword. Both sought to keep their metaphysics warm, to paraphrase T.S. Eliot, by turning to the Elizabethans, Rickword perhaps for the satiric energy of the age, while Crane was attracted to their burnished, luminous forms. Both poets were conscious of publishing under regimes of censorship (*The Calendar* had published one of the first critical studies of the Marquis de Sade). Crane's poetry demonstrates his dances with Comstock in such coded poems as his elegy for Oscar Wilde 'C33', and in 'Voyages', which dwells on his relationship with Emil Opffer, and even his depiction of cruising in 'The Tunnel' ('searching, thumbing the midnight on the piers'). Rickword satirises puritanical attitudes to literature in poems such as 'The Handmaid of Religion':

> Neither barbarians nor malaria
> destroyed Rome's grip on her vast area,
> but naughty novels sold in shops
> unhindered by censorious cops.

Each of Crane's 'Three Songs' published by Rickword are erotic, with 'Southern Cross' mixing spiritual strains with more earthly stirrings, while 'National Winter Garden' and 'Virginia' are, like Rickword's 'pornology' in 'The Handmaid of Religion', burlesques on sexual mores. In fact, one of the often overlooked elements of Crane's poetry is its bawdy humour:

> Outspoken buttocks in pink beads
> Invite the necessary cloudy clinch
> Of bandy eyes...No extra mufflings here:
> The world's one flagrant, sweating cinch
> ('National Winter Garden')

Intriguingly, both Crane and Rickword wrote variations on the Faust legend, and Rickword was clearly drawn to the daemonic poet in Crane, man enough to be damned in his attempts to 'lend a myth to God'. Crane sent Rickword his 'For the Marriage of Faustus and Helen' (first published in magazines between 1923-1924), which Rickword admired. Rickword's own 'Theme for *The Pseudo-Faustus*' appeared in his 1928 collection, *Invocation to Angels*. Faust seems to offer both poets a means of conceptualizing freedom beyond the policed horizons of the Twenties:

> *There is the world dimensional for*
> *those untwisted by the love of things*
> *irreconcilable...*
> ('For the Marriage of Faustus and Helen')

> Deprived of freedom in time, space and love,
> they seek enfranchisement in the air beyond
> the city's silent rows of gnawing roofs
> ('Theme for *The Pseudo-Faustus*')

By contrast, Rickword's received other poems by Crane with cautious praise. Along with 'Three Songs', Crane had submitted 'Cutty Sark', 'The Harbor Dawn' and 'O Carib Isle', noting the importance of the visual arrangement of 'Cutty Sark'. It was, he wrote, 'a "cartogram", if one may designate a special use of the calligramme. The "ships" should meet and pass in line and type – as well as in wind and memory', a 'phantom regatta seen from Brooklyn Bridge'. Rickword accepted 'Three Songs' and 'O Carib Isle' (although after the *transition* printed the latter, he declined the poem). His letter added, '[t]he other poems I am returning. I think your poetry is unique when it hovers on the knife-edge between illumination and disintegration. The other poems seem to me a trifle on the wrong side'.

The 'wrong side' of Crane's poetry was, for Rickword, its feints with surrealism. Rickword had briefly studied French literature at Oxford, and he and Crane shared an interest in French symbolist poetry. Rickword's *Rimbaud: The Boy and the Poet* had been published in 1924, and

Crane wrote to him: 'I found so much in your Rimbaud volume which was sympathetic and critically stimulating.' Nevertheless, Rickword did not at that time share Crane's interest in surrealism. Although he later described his dismissal of surrealism as 'positively frumpish', in 1925, he had reviewed André Breton's *Manifeste Du Surréalisme: Poisson Solube*, asserting that Breton 'ignores altogether the constructive effort in poetry, the organisation of the whole into something significant', comments which also shed light on Rickword's rejection of some of the fragments of *The Bridge*, which he viewed as disparate, fractured parts of a forthcoming long poem.

NOTE
Grateful acknowledgement for use of unpublished letters between Crane and Rickword to Hart Crane Papers, Rare Book and Manuscript Library, Columbia University Special Collections (New York).

Three Poems

J AMES W OMACK

Anekdot

Another city poem, another anecdote.
St Petersburg. The band we saw that evening
Was Полтора Кило Отличного Пюре,[1] which translates as
A Kilo and a Half of Excellent Mashed Potatoes.
Jeez, lighten up; it was the millennium, Jesus.

Sample lyrics: 'I walk through my
native microregion | hacking at
lapdogs with a large axe.' Where are they now,
would be a fair question. Even Russia
can't sustain all types of cynicism forever.

A basement red-brick, with a crammed bar –
a little bit ayurvedic café, a little bit
cult HQ – and while Jeremy went to *blue
with the dickstickers*, which translates as
whatever the hell you want it to mean,

I drank there with you, and it was almost erotic.
Although mostly it was pornographic:
a crammed bar, and no one caring.
When you said *let's get out of here*,
I asked *why* and you shrugged. *Fair point.*

People went through and disappeared
from our lives back then, hostels and beds.
When a few years later I found myself
in your Berlin, I wrote you a long Leonard
Cohen-y email, which I don't think you

ever answered. Spam folder, perhaps.
Friends of friends sent me rumours
but even those petered out, bored:
did you get hoovered/god/a wife/true
communism on earth. Delete as inappropriate.

I moved on. Yeah, I'm totally all over
all this. This is my life, nor am I out of it:
I'm a shark, sleek and total, dead-eyed.
Where am I now, is always the only question.
Jeez, it was the millennium. Lighten up. Jeez-o.

---

1 The band's name is pronounced *Poltorá Kiló Otlíchnovo Piuré.*

Two Public Schoolboys, Walking Over Skeletons

When the first snows came we changed our walk to work
for certain definitions of work, for certain definitions of walking:
we skiddered the mile downhill to the grey-block Philology building
with its lagged-pipe smell and mildly lecherous faculty.

Moscow was savage that winter: they devalued the currency,
but that didn't make us, dollar supported, any the richer
(it's no use having money if the shops sell only vodka and cheese)
and we lost weight and walked rather than spend 20 roubles bussing it.

The snows were thick and sudden and the city changed with them,
became more purposeful, sadder, more of itself, stank less,
and somehow yes, it's what snow does, more innocent.
Snow is a useful stand-in for actual innocence.

So we slid on packed snow and ice for months from November
and taught our classes and explained grammar via Dylan lyrics
to somehow resentful students who were gulpingly avid to learn
but also seemed upset that they had to submit to learn from us.

There were plus points, like when I was left at home for an evening,
and the whole filthy flat was mine for a few hours,
so I read a little while, then put on the Ella Fitzgerald cassette,
and heard 'Love for Sale' as snow fell against the orange streetlights.

But interactions with real people, discussions, humanity...
they all went on in their bearable, slightly angry fashion:
the snow covering things up till you forgot about them,
grew angry again, learnt more, waited for more snow.

When the thaw kicked in, maybe round April, a month before exams,
we carried on walking by what we still called the new route.
One day in the slush something cracked under my feet:
I looked down on a stray dog's white ribcage, skull grin, some hair.

Two public schoolboys, walking over skeletons.
More and more corpses came to light as the snows receded.
We were going to leave the country, so what could we do?
What we did was just that: leave and remember so little.

'She told me this story ...'

She told me this story: in a different flat
one late spring day, a swift fell into her bedroom.
It lay still and scared, breathing fast and still.

Telling the story, a slave's inspiration, she knelt
to the floor, her wrists pinioned behind her back
to show how the swift had fallen.

It progressed, how she had scooped the bird
into her resolute hands and held it unresisting
to the window, how it had been thrown out

and failed to fly, how it had fallen down the well
between the flats, and landed neatly,
and lain waiting for the local cat.

How she had run downstairs, knocked on every door
until an old Chinese woman had let her climb
through a ground floor window onto the tiles

(the Chinese woman was never seen again,
had maybe never existed), how she had carried
the bird upstairs in her hands without spilling it.

And this second time, how she had held the swift
further out, waited for it to unship its wings, how it had
scrabblingly launched itself to a world it understood.

(The next time she gave me this story,
she was with her then boyfriend,
and he was telling her not to help.)

W.D. Snodgrass on Jarrell and Frost

Two Unpublished Letters

EDITED BY JEFFREY MEYERS

THE POET W.D. SNODGRASS (1926–2009) was born in Pennsylvania, served in the wartime Navy, studied with Robert Lowell at the University of Iowa in 1947–51 and with Randall Jarrell at the University of Colorado summer school in 1951. He was a fellow guest with Robert Frost at the Washington, D.C. Poetry Festival during the Cuban missile crisis in October 1962. Snodgrass won the Pulitzer Prize for his first book, *Heart's Needle* (1959), a tender and intricate account of a father's divorce and separation from his daughter. This book influenced the confessional poetry of Lowell's *Life Studies*, Anne Sexton's *To Bedlam and Part Way Back* and Sylvia Plath's *The Colossus*. Snodgrass taught for many years at Cornell, Rochester, Wayne State, Syracuse and Delaware.

When I was writing *Manic Power: Robert Lowell and His Circle* (1987) and *Robert Frost: A Biography* (1996), I asked Snodgrass for biographical information. He generously provided this in two typed, single-spaced, brilliantly perceptive and amusing letters. The first letter, 2 December 1981, three-and-a-half pages, discusses Randall Jarrell's complex connections with women, his serious interest in tennis, effective teaching, relations with students, useful tuition of and cruel attacks on Snodgrass as well as Jarrell's first and second wives, and other sources of information. The second letter, 24 September 1994, two-and-a-half pages, analyses Robert Frost's competitive streak, suicide themes, appearance at the Washington Poetry Festival, Jarrell's and Richard Blackmur's negative response to him, Frost's destructive joy, his soliciting three ovations and Snodgrass' reaction.

*

308 Delaware Circle
Newark, Delaware 19711
2 December, 1981

Jeffrey Meyers
2005 Glenwood
Boulder, Colorado 80302

Dear Professor Meyers,

I must apologize for the long delay in answering your letter; unfortunately, when I left my summer place in New York state in August a number of letters became misplaced and have only now surfaced again. I am sorry that your letter was among those which were temporarily lost.

I shall be happy to tell you anything I can about Randall Jarrell, though it would be a help to me if you could tell me in greater detail what sort of thing you would like to know. You ask particularly about him as 'teacher, tennis player and ladies man'. The second two of these categories I can handle rather quickly, but the first will take more time and space. I believe that when Jarrell came to Boulder in 1951 his marriage with Mackie had already broken up. Indeed, I may be responsible for his getting together with Mary. She came to me during the first couple of days and asked me who she should take courses with and I told her by all means Jarrell. They began going out almost at once and spent a great deal of time together during that conference. If he showed other signs of being a ladies man, either then or in the period when I knew him later, I'm not aware of it; he seemed to be very much married and since I, at first, disliked both of them I thought they were good enough for each other. (My feelings later changed about this.) I have heard that Jarrell was involved with another young lady at the time of his nervous breakdown, which entailed considerable trouble with Mary, and I believe I have met a young lady who hinted that she was the person in question – but since all of this is vague in my memory and mere hearsay at best I think it might be best ignored.

When I first met Jarrell there, I asked if he might like to play some tennis. He replied that he might, but that he should caution me that he was very good and he wouldn't want to play if I couldn't give him a stiff game. I felt rather insulted by that but it may have been for the best – he shortly found a partner in another department who was able to challenge him as I surely wouldn't have been. We did play some ping-pong where I think I challenged him rather more than he liked. I suspect that he won that too, however, as he became quite anxious to win and I have always found that difficult to oppose.

The teaching, as I say, will be more difficult to describe. Jarrell was viewed there, both as a person and as a teacher, with a strange combination of awe and suspicion. His girlish manner astounded everyone. One would find him lounging about on a stone wall somewhere wearing elegant tennis shorts and exclaiming, 'Gee! Golly! Don't you just love it here! I think it's just dovey!!!' This is quite literal. I was as astonished as anyone else, feeling that this was the one man serious enough to have viewed a horror like World War II and been able to actually write about it. The sense of distrust and disquiet became even more pointed in his classes because he chose not to handle the student poems all the time (at this distance I can't recall if he ever handled any of them in the class) but instead did analyses of such classics as 'Frankie and Johnny' and Frost's 'The Witch of Coos'. These analyses, however, were so extremely brilliant, entertaining and illuminating that criticism was stifled. For myself, I have stolen these lectures of his and delivered them to my own classes at any opportunity! The general disapproval of Jarrell broke into the open when, on the occasion that it had been announced he would give a reading of his poems, he substituted a reading from his novel *Pictures from an Institution*. Though I came to like it later, the novel certainly did not seem very good then, but I cannot now say whether that is why he later rewrote it. He may have given a second reading to quiet this uproar; I can't now recall.

I was far from Jarrell's favorite student there though he did finally allow that I was 'some good'. There was one student, from New York I believe, whose work he liked quite a lot. I remember also that he was particularly taken with the poems of a very elderly lady whose story is somewhat interesting. The student body there was made up of two sharply divided groups: the college-age people like myself who provided most of the writing vigor and the older people, mostly women, who provided most of the money since they were not on fellowships as we were. The one person who broke this pattern was the elderly woman in question – some years before her husband had died and, being left at odd ends, she took a job for the government which sent her as a stenographer for court cases to Okinawa. This was a shattering experience for her: the things that she saw happening in army court martials brought all of her dearest beliefs into question. She became at least as sceptical as we younger people were. Jarrell said that her poems about these cases were good and that one in particular had moved him almost to tears. It was very poignant watching her balanced between the two groups while the older people tried to coax her back into their more comfortable position. I rather believe that she went and at her age I suppose it is better that way.

His treatment of my own work was extremely brutal. I brought with me a group of poems which had been praised quite highly by such people as Robert Penn Warren, Cleanth Brooks, John Crowe Ransom, and Robert Lowell. He and I would sit on one of the verandas there at the dormitory in Boulder and he would read me lines from these poems and simply howl with laughter. I recall him slapping his knees, throwing his head back and howling, 'Snodgrass! You wrote that! Listen! Listen to this . . . .' You can imagine that this was extremely upsetting. At the same time, I have to say that he was right and in the long run he had a very salutary effect on my poems. I cannot say that I like the way he did it but I could not finally be other than grateful to him. I had been very much under the influence of those other teachers I mentioned earlier and of the poets that influenced them – the English Metaphysicals and the French symbolistes. He helped to move me in a direction I was already going because of certain other influences and much more in the direction of poets such as Hardy and Frost. The only piece of mine that he liked that I brought along there was a translation of Ovid's *Metamorphoses*. (I am not sure whether any of the poems that he disapproved of have appeared in print –I have a suspicion that 'Orpheus' and the poem with the Greek title in my first volume might have been in the sheet I gave him.)

I might say that he came to like some of my poems considerably and we came to be on somewhat more amiable terms. All the same, it was never safe to voice an opinion which differed from his. I recall that after the Boulder conference he came to give a lecture or reading at Iowa City and visited me there. I don't believe I have ever been quite so savagely attacked in my own home.

Some years later when Robert Lowell's play *Benito Cereno* appeared at the American Place Theatre in New York he came to me on the stage afterwards and said, 'That's the best play ever written in American, isn't it?'. I ventured to say that I thought it was a very fine play but not so great as that and again received a most vicious insult. One usually ignored these insults partly because they were often delivered in terms so witty that one was too weak with laughing to reply; at other times because one was so aghast at being attacked so brutally that one couldn't reply. Again, perhaps one doubted one's ability to match him at this sort of thing.

That is perhaps enough for now though I'll be glad to try to answer any other more specific questions that might be on your mind. Do let me say how pleased I am that you are doing this biography. There is no American poet so unjustly neglected (unless it be his hero John Crowe Ransom) and it is certainly time that someone tried to redress this balance. Incidentally, I hope that you know how this neglect has come about – have you heard the story about how he came to be excluded from Oscar Williams's anthologies? He told me about this himself and I'll be glad to pass it on if it will be of interest to you.

With all best wishes,
[signed] W. D. Snodgrass

P.S. Please forgive the typos and corrections – I have a new typist.

P.S. It occurs to me that there are several other things that I might mention which could be of use to you. First of all, I said that I thought that Randall and Mackie had broken up at the time he came to Colorado. This is also, apparently, the time when Mary's first marriage had broken up. My impression is that the actual divorce proceedings had not begun but that she had definitely decided to end the marriage; I do recall her getting quite a number of frantic telephone calls from California, some of them from her daughter but some of them, I believe, from her about-to-be 'ex'.

I should say that it seems to me very unlikely that Jarrell would ever give the impression of being a ladies man; it was much too important to him to give the appearance of being blissfully wedded. Around the Women's College of North Carolina where he and Mackie both taught, there were stories about the two of them holding hands and skipping across the campus or sitting in the back row of the movie house necking, only the day before their divorce became final!

Finally I would suggest that if you would like to get some corroboration on any of these points (I am fairly doubtful of my own memory) you might drop notes to Richard Snyder and Dominick Consolo both of whom then were writing and who were my closest friends there. Since that time, both are teaching and I believe that Dick now writes only poems; he teaches at Ashtabula in Ohio while Dom teaches at Denison University there.

[signed] W. D. Snodgrass

Snodgrass' modest, sympathetic and incisive comments, made before creative writing classes became pandemic, were written as carefully as his published essays. They provide precious insights about the sexual seductions at literary conferences, Jarrell's athletic and poetic rivalry, and the girlish and cruel sides of his character. His howling with laughter recalls Ford Madox Ford rolling on the floor for emphasis when criticizing Pound's Canzoni.

W. D. Snodgrass
R.D. #1, Box 51
Erieville, NY 13061
Sept. 24, 1994

Dear Jeffrey Meyers,

Thanks for your note of Sept. 8. I'm afraid that I only met Frost once though it could be said that I had a 'run-in' with him on another occasion when we didn't meet. I had almost no 'personal relations' with him. I thought him (and still do) our best poet excluding only Whitman. I had heard enough unpleasant stories about him, though, that I didn't expect to like him and wasn't anxious to meet him. So far as I know he didn't respond (directly) to me either as a man or as a poet. On the other hand, I don't think he was 'primarily responsible for introducing the sense of competition among American poets'. I always assumed that was active long before his time – though now that you suggest it, I suppose he may have given it a sort of currency if not of respectability. I myself think that competition is very important and helpful when it's held in check. Most of the best poets I have known, while they may be jealous of other poets' achievements and/or awards, will turn that jealousy to something creative by giving one another honest and helpful criticism. I've seldom seen the kind of envious hindrance which Frost often enough threw in others' way.

My 'run-in' with Frost happened while I was teaching at Wayne State Univ. in Detroit. When Frost came there for a reading, some of my students must have got hold of him before his appearance and asked him about their teacher's idea that 'Stopping by Woods' had something to do with suicide. During his reading, he talked about how scandalous it was that certain academics would say such things about him and his work. I don't recall now whether he said what he thought the poem was about. However, the next day he appeared in Ann Arbor, Mich. about forty miles away and there he read the poem again; friends who were present told me that after reading it, he looked up startled and said, 'Well, now, that does have a good deal of the ultimate about it, doesn't it?'. Is it possible that he really had forgotten – he wrote about suicide so obviously elsewhere; my teacher, Paul Engle, spent hours on the beaches of Cuba talking him out of it after his son committed suicide; he so often used the threat of suicide to get his own way with others like Mrs. Morrison!

Not too long after that, I believe, I heard him read at a big poetry festival in Washington at the time of the Cuban missile crisis. At that time I was introduced to him but we had almost nothing to say to each other. Meantime, the crisis was mounting, Jackie Kennedy had cancelled our lunch with her (she was reportedly hidden in a cave somewhere) and we all expected to be blown into bits within hours.

When I left the room where I met Frost, I was with a young lady I scarcely knew though it appeared we were having an affair; I did not discourage this appearance.

We were taken to dinner at Trader Vic's by a reporter from *Time* or *Newsweek* – a less than noble event – an appearance of illicit relations, the expensive phony food of a tourist trap, all paid for by the plastic card of a man from a magazine I didn't respect but whose praise I wanted. Meantime, you could hear Jack Kennedy on the TV upstairs saying that unfortunately we might have to discontinue western civilization (or eastern, for that matter).

Frost's reading that night was the big event of the conference, which was mostly disgraceful – all the poetry politicians applauding each other's sorry work. I recall Randall Jarrell, who had just seen a BBC girl carrying a Nagra tape recorder to one of the readings, saying that he and his wife would tackle and hold her if I would just disappear with the recorder – no record of the event must ever get out of the country. The one saving grace of those several days was John Berryman's first really public reading of the 'Dream Songs'.

In any case, I arrived at Frost's reading quite drunk – the young lady was wearing some gardenias fished out of our massive bowl of booze (and I may well have been, too). Frost, within several months of his death, not only read a poem of Robinson Jeffers, 'Shine, Perishing Republic', but also made an improvised addition to one of his own – referring to the current crisis with a clear air of triumph. (I wrote a piece about this that appeared in the Spring 1994 Paris Review – you could look up the poem there if you're interested; I don't have any of the materials here with me now.) A generous interpretation might say that he was exhilarated by the air of confrontation and that he saw the crisis as a refutation of his liberal critics, a proof that the direct assertion and/or threat of physical force (even to the extent of nuclear war) WAS the right way to handle the international conflict. That probably was a part of it. But some of the remarks he made suggested that he was also glad that now he would not have to die alone – and that, moreover, we would die without having the full career he'd had. He ad-libbed at one point, 'Well, you didn't want to just fade out, did you? Why not go out in a blaze of glory?'. Truly cold-blooded mockery; meantime, he kept holding on to the lectern and pumping his body up and down as if with laughter.

The audience, however, seemed so pre-tuned to reverence that all this passed over their heads. Only Richard Blackmur (who was sitting several rows ahead of me) took this as I did – he was vigorously cursing Frost in no very soft voice. When Frost was finished, the audience gave him the obligatory standing ovation and started out. Whereupon, he got up and went back to the podium and called everyone back while he made some inconsequential remarks. Once again, he received a standing ovation and again the audience started out. And, once again, he called them back so they had to give him a third standing ovation!

As the young lady and I threaded our way out through the worshipful crowd, I heard myself loudly singing one of the Scottish ballads, 'The Baron o' Brackley':

> She was trantin' and dancin' and singin' for joy;
> She vowed that very night she would feast Inverey.
> She hae lach wi' him, drunk wi' him, carried him ben;
> She was kind wi' the villain that had slain her good man.

I couldn't imagine why I was behaving so badly; only the next day did I recognize the song as an index of how thoroughly betrayed I felt by Frost's attitude – above all by his glee that we all might soon 'go out in a blaze of glory' – which he saw as coinciding with his own moment of glory.

Forgive me if I report this in such detail but I thought that since this was a fairly climactic event in his career, you might get a number of reports on it and I'm sure my view of it will be at variance with most.

Meanwhile, I hope this may prove of some use. While you were in Casenovia [doing research on Edmund Wilson] (only about 10 miles away) I wish you had contacted us – it would have been good to get together.

With all best wishes,
[signed] W. D. Snodgrass

Snodgrass was apprehensive about meeting Frost, who had once threatened to commit suicide and disliked his dark interpretation of 'Stopping by Woods on a Snowy Evening'. There was an electrically charged tension during the missile crisis. Frost had just met Khrushchev in Moscow in September 1962 and seemed to relish the apocalyptic atmosphere. Jackie Kennedy was hidden away, but the poets continued to drink heavily and flatter each other. Despite Frost's great fame, he still craved and encouraged more adulation.

Published with the kind permission of Kathleen Snodgrass.

50 Chicagos for Paul Fournel

PHILIP TERRY

The chicago is a poetic form created by Paul Fournel, President of Oulipo (the *Ouvroir de littérature potentielle*, or Workhop of Poetential Literature), which bears a family resemblance to the riddle. It consists of a single stanza of five lines: the final line is a homophonic translation of a place name (or of the name of a person, a cheese, etc.); the first four lines are homosyntactic translations, or variants, of the final line, the 'solution' to the riddle, which is held in abeyance for the reader to guess. The final line of one of Fournel's inaugural texts was a deformation of 'Chicago' – '*Chie cagot*' (literally 'shit sanctimonious hypocrite') – which led Oulipo to name the form a *chicago*.

1.
Brassed off K
Fed up L
Sprightly M
Enthusiastic N
....

2.
Six win
Seven take a licking
Five draw
Three default
....

3.
John Vauxhall
Pete Volvo
Mike BMW
Rich Peugeot
....

4.
Fashionable slang
Out of date patois
Cool pidgin
Hip lingo
....

5.
Pout vanished
Smile reappeared
Brooding terminated
Mourning prolonged
....

6.
Notch centimetre
Sign foot
Varnish mile
Stain millimetre
....

7.
Girl elbow him
Boy knee her
Woman tongue him
Child eye them
....

8.
Restaurants a socialite
Cafés a writer
Wine bars a womaniser
Bistros a gourmand
....

9.
More plausible K
More realistic L
Newer M
Better N
....

10.
Moo wind
Meow snow
Woof sleet
Cockadoodledoo thunder
....

11.
Hide shares
Dismantle fair
Close superstore
Open boot sale
....

12.
Meat distributor
Egg farmer
Chicken plucker
Poultry feeder
....

13.
Macintosh minnow
Burberry bream
Poncho pilchard
Duffelcoat dab
....

14.
Mind bush
Cerebellum shrub
Thought hedge
Head flower
....

15.
John
Netty
Bog
Shithouse
....

16.
Peaceful deposit
Buddhist extract
Mindful substrata
Chilled mineral
....

17.
Microphone stands
Pedals
Picks
Guitars
....

18.
Letter when
Text why
Email what
Telegram but
....

19.
Grass cuts
Hedges prickle
Fields bite
Fences snag
....

20.
Divircee consumed them
Former lover swallowed it
Cast off drank him
Old flame chewed us
....

21.
Kidney puddle
Heart lake
Lung tarn
Pancreas river
....

22.
Christ nuisance
Mohammed plague
God boon
Shiva storm
....

23.
Knocker quick
Buzzer stuck
Alarm loud
Intercom slow
....

24.
King pound
Princess kilogram
Queen ounce
Emperor gram
....

25.
Bounder isn't
Boor was
Misanthrope wasn't
Pretender can't
....

26.
Lichen PLC
Grass Inc.
Heather Associates
Tundra & Sons
....

27.
Fuck blood
Inseminate remains
Shag mess
Screw gut
....

28.
Heaven stun A
Earth eat B
Sea swallow C
Sky conceal D
....

29.
John pound 9
Kim yen 40
Pedro peseta 7
Luigi lire 1
....

30.
Peregrinate
Wander
Travel
Escape
....

31.
Bright sun scythe
Black rain turn
Luminescent mist
hover
Dull wind break
....

32.
Done B
Undone C
Done E
Undone A
....

33.
Cotton foot
Glass ear
Tin heart
Rubber jaw
....

34.
Prostitute fake
Sex worker pretence
Courtesan deceit
Escort deception
....

35.
Texted director
Emailed cameraman
Booked theatre
Met funders
....

36.
Purse mum
Box auntie
Container gran
Suitcase cousin
....

37.
Pastille Ken's
Jelly baby Sam's
Polo Jane's
Gobstopper Bill's
....

38.
Egg whip bridge
Steak knead road
Ice cream boil tunnel
Pasta grill flyover
....

39.
Giant peach bark
Small blackberry whisper
Medium-sized melon yell
Long cucumber spit
....

40.
Olive branch
Pear trunk
Fig leaf
Apple fruit
....

41.
Water cleanse
Soup appetise
Coffee stimulate
Mint refresh
....

42.
Body in
Corpse out
Stiff under
Skeleton between
....

43.
Napoleon daguerrotype
Rommel photograph
Patton portrait
Cromwell etching
....

44.
Ruin door
Spoil exit
Smash portal
Splinter portcullis
....

45.
H see *do*
I salute *ré*
J lose *mi*
K trip *fa*
....

46.
Snort Apollo
Inject Neptune
Drink Narcissus
Swallow Daphne
....

47.
Gran Lomond
Teen Neagh
Lad Fyne
Lass Rannoch
....

48.
Prayer deceived
Eucharist trumped
Confirmation cancelled
Confession fudged
....

49.
Bus station inertia
Taxi rank hussle
Airport search
Station crush
....

50.
Refuelled: yes
Took off: yes
Radio contact: yes
Reached destination: yes
....

1. Bordeaux (Bored O)
2. Toulouse (Two lose)
3. Bradford (Brad Ford)
4. Chicago (Chic argot)
5. Saigon (Sigh gone)
6. Markinch (Mark inch)
7. Manchester (Man chest her)
8. Barcelona (Bars a loner)
9. Truro (Truer O)
10. Bahrain (Baah rain)
11. Stowmarket (Stow market)
12. Fishguard (Fish guard)
13. Cape Cod (Cape cod)
14. Braintree (Brain tree)
15. Looe (Loo)
16. Zennor (Zen ore)
17. Leeds (Leads)
18. Cardiff (Card if)
19. Hastings (Hay stings)
20. Exeter (Ex ate her)
21. Liverpool (Liver pool)
22. Budapest (Buddha pest)
23. Belfast (Bell fast)
24. Princeton (Prince ton)
25. Cadiz (Cad is)
26. Moscow (Moss Co.)
27. Bangor (Bang gore)
28. Helsinki (Hell sink E)
29. Timbuctoo (Tim buck 2)
30. Rome (Roam)
31. Palermo (Pale air mow)
32. Dundee (Done D)
33. Leatherhead (Leather head)
34. Horsham (Whore sham)
35. Rangoon (Rang goon)
36. Baghdad (Bag dad)
37. Los Angeles (Losange Ellie's)
38. Amsterdam (Ham stir dam)
39. Minneaplois (Mini apple hiss)
40. Beirut (Bay root)
41. Deauville (Dough fill)
42. Carcassone (Carcass on)
43. Montevideo (Monty video)
44. Margate (Marr gate)
45. El Paso (L pass *so*)
46. Tokyo (Toke Io)
47. Totnes (Tot Ness)
48. Maastricht (Mass tricked)
49. Portrush (Port rush)
50. Llandudno (Landed: no)

'A Sighting'
© Michael Augustin, 2020

Aftergrass

Jane Clarke, *When the Tree Falls*
(Bloodaxe), £9.95

Reviewed by SUE LEIGH

Jane Clarke grew up on a farm in Roscommon and now lives in Glenmalure, County Wicklow. Both her first book, *The River* (2015), and this, her second, are rooted in rural life. Loss is never far away in her work but neither is delight – in the natural world, people, the particular quality of a place. She writes with clarity, spareness and lyrical intensity. (The poems are largely written in simple two- or three-line stanzas.) And her voice, as Anne Enright has said, 'slips into the Irish tradition with such ease it is as though she had always been at the heart of it'.

There is an acceptance in *When the Tree Falls* of the rhythm of things: birth, death, regrowth and renewal. At its heart is an elegiac sequence for the poet's father in which she reflects on the time of his illness and death, mourning him and moving on. Many of these poems draw on the daily life of the farm – 'his time is precious as a dry spell / when there's silage to be cut' – and at night when he is ill 'old hurts / and worries surface / like stones in a well-tilled field'. After his death the poet recalls her father's voice in the names of the fields and his whistling in the call of the curlew. 'Aftergrass' also raises environmental concerns as she describes after a heatwave 'shallows more shallow / than we've ever seen' and imagines telling her dead father that 'the sun has scorched / every blade of grass'.

There are poems about other relationships too. The complexity of that between mother and daughter is considered with honesty in 'The trouble' as she wonders 'how to forgive / the one to whom / you owe too much'. (That 'too' is telling.) A memory of her mother using paper patterns in dressmaking recalls a time 'when we believed / if I followed the map / I could be / whoever I wanted to be'. Coming out was challenging at a time when 'we had to claim / a space for love in the half-hidden places'. In 'Point of Departure' the poet speaks of the difficulty her mother has in accepting her identity: 'her heart / is broken over what I have told her'. But there is excitement too in this new freedom, as 'a gate opens / into a meadow I have never seen'.

Clarke, although deeply connected to her past, is part of a new, more inclusive and compassionate Ireland. Two important referendums have been part of that opening up: the right of same-sex couples to marry and the provision that may be made by law for the termination of pregnancy. 'Polling Station' relates to the latter as 'neighbours welcome sunshine after the wettest / of wet winters' and 'every family has stories'. There are poems too relating to the first, about a time when gay relationships were a source of stigma. In 'Glasnevin', a poem inspired by Elizabeth O'Farrell and Julia Grenan, two nurses and

couriers in the Easter Rising of 1916, the poet questions the wording on their grave, '*faithful comrade, lifelong friend*'. Did the words say enough, she wonders.

There are also moving elegies for Clarke's friend, Shirley McClure. 'Copper Soles' recalls a Finnish story in which the hero needs copper soles on his shoes to complete a number of tasks. 'Dear friend', the poet then says, 'while the doctors chase pain / around your body, / where will we find such a cobbler?' As she sits by her friend's bedside, the speaker remembers when they were swimming together in the river that stretched before them 'until illness seeped in, / stealthy as groundwater after a storm'. And when her friend was surfing in 'the time outside time / when you catch the gust / and are swept the full length of the fetch'.

Unsettling the Sublime

Mona Arshi, *Dear Big Gods*. £9.99;
Janette Ayachi, *Hand Over Mouth Music* (both Liverpool), £9.99

Reviewed by HAL COASE

What can a poet do with nature? The question itself hardly belongs in our young, unhappy anthropocene. It is almost a trespass. Full of hubristic presumption, it suggests a tarnished model for thinking about poetry and the environment, one junked and discarded in a not-so-distant past age that is still, nonetheless, littering contemporary thinking. Mona Arshi's second collection, *Dear Big Gods*, is at its best when it struggles against the assumptions of nature poetry. These are poems that mostly do nothing 'with' nature. Rather, they trace a fraught conversation between their lyric subjects and their environments. It's a collection that gains its strengths not from the devices of ecopoetry (nothing here, in short, that speaks 'for' or 'to' nature) but through a tenacious exploration of where the need to use (and abuse) natural metaphors might come from and what we might be left with when they fail us. In its most arresting moments, as in 'Autumn Epistles', mid-way through the collection, Arshi constructs curling, measured stanzas that unsettle the sublime and depict thought itself as a plaything of the world around it:

> I bend myself right back
> to breath-filled knowing again,
> the dormant mumble
>   of well-water and the implied
> lakes in our mind we
> never hesitate to still.

The 'breath-filled knowing' of poetry is a refuge of sorts but nothing about this interiority is steady or certain: the moves between images are hesitant, restless – 'implied' is the perfect word to note hanging at the poem's end.

There is much else probed by Arshi across a varied collection other than this question of how to present, how to 'get at' the natural world within the space of a lyric poem. Yet what's remarkable is how insistently this theme returns, as if the natural world – lending an image, then intruded upon, then ransacked for metaphor – can keep demanding that it take centre stage, that it do something with its presence in a poem to knock the steady centeredness of the lyric-self. The opening sequence of poems, for example, are insistently literal steps into nature: 'This time I'm a wren'; 'This is what a flower does'; 'you naked as a bird' – slim, measured lines that inhabit metamorphic states so as to reflect on the transformative potentials of faith, grief and prayer. But by the time we reach 'Now I know the Truth about Octopuses (and the lies we tell our children)' something has shifted. The choppy form here suggests that the gulf between the natural world and interiority cannot be so straightforwardly bridged. Indeed, the entire poem speaks to the inscrutability of nature, the sheer otherness of natural 'Truths' that put them well past knowing. This, ultimately, is the question arising across Arshi's work: how can we re-mystify the natural world without distancing ourselves from it?

Janette Ayachi's first collection, *Hand Over Mouth Music*, ranging across the Mediterranean from Algeria to the Adriatic (as well as all over Scotland), takes an equal interest in this question. The fine, precise sketches of landscapes and settings – Annaba, Glasgow, Edinburgh, St Kilda – are rendered with such formal precision and metrical adroitness that it's only when read right through that they seem to collectively raise difficult questions about what it might mean to belong somewhere, to be held in a place and to be given a space to breath. Each one of these settings is troubled by what Margaret Ronda has termed 'remainders': those things (emotional, literary or material) left over from former productive modes that ecopoetry can force us to confront. When Ayachi asks us to dwell in a place, we are shown the historical detritus that has formed it and we sense how fragile the privilege of simply staying put might be. Ayachi registers that fragility in 'the distance in between' the places we pass through and the positions we speak from, renewing the theme each time the poem's themselves travel on elsewhere. Then again, there is much in these poems to sit with – as 'Delta of Italy' has it: 'Who can resist / Such a stasis / Of healing chrysalis', even if that 'resist' intimates this might be the easy way to avoid confronting hard truths.

The hardest truth here, grimly inevitable, is ecological collapse. It is in the longer poems, in particular, that Ayachi is able to 'listen to the world and its breaking down of things' ('I Laughed So Much I Lost My Voice'), to bring to the fore the terrible, matter-of-fact reality of climate change. The sharply framed vignettes of far-flung places are all united by the distress wrought on them by this reality, as though, like Julian Charrière's photographs of the lush beaches of the Bikini Atoll, they are damaged and burnt by the lethal material sunk around their beautiful scenery. These collections are, like Charrière's work, not pursuing a polemic or even adopting a consistent attitude to the natural world. But they do both think hard about how the natural can be rendered in today's world. And whilst they may each end on a note of prayer and a plea for calm, before arriving there, any reader will be unsettled by their not-so-scenic routes.

The Just with the Unjust

Anthony Anaxagorou, *After the Formalities* (Penned in the Margins), £9.99

Reviewed by EVAN JONES

On Tuesday 17 February 1959, the plane carrying the Turkish Prime Minister to talks concerning the Cyprus affair crashed just before landing in London. Adnan Menderes survived and was found in a tree by a local farmer, who offered first aid and a cup of tea.

Cyprus had been a colony of Great Britain since 1878, though different groups over the years had pressured for that to change. This came to the forefront of world politics first in the 1950s, when Greek terrorists (EOKA) began bombing the British and the Turks – and Turkish terrorists (TMT) countered. There were calls for independence, for *enosis* (reunion) with the nation of Greece from the Cypriots and reciprocal attacks on the ethnic Greeks still living in mainland Turkey. The three interested parties agreed to meet in London: the Greeks, led by Prime Minister Konstantinos Karamanlis; the Turks, led by Menderes; the Cypriots, represented by the Ethnarch, Markarios III. But it was the British who took the most away from the conference, seeing to it that no one was satisfied. One of those present at the negotiations was the Greek ambassador to the UK, George Seferiades, known better by his *nom de plume*, Seferis. He wrote to his sister, Ioanna: 'I have the feeling that this time it's not just Cyprus but the fate of Greece itself that's hanging in the balance. And behind all that there is a Nemesis which has already begun to work; a Nemesis that, in the way of these things, strikes down the just with the unjust.'

Seferis was very much for *enosis* but was sidelined by his own prime minister before and during the negotiations. He tried to warn his government and Markarios that the British had something else in mind. He was, in retrospect, entirely correct: Greece did the worst out of the negotiations and the Nemesis he referred to condemned the island. Cyprus became a republic, independent. Within fifteen years it was partitioned. The Cypriots maintain their section, the Turks theirs, and Great Britain has a Mediterranean military base of operations.

Perhaps *enosis* was never going to work. The Cypriots remain outsiders, even among the Greeks. Their heritage is viewed as hybridised and messy; they are the butt of jokes: a Greek, an Englishman and a Cypriot walk into a bar. The Cypriot does not come off well. If people think now of Cyprus, it is a holiday destination, all-inclusive and affordable.

The experiences Anthony Anaxagorou describes in *After the Formalities* begin here, as refugees who have fled the violence and insurrection in Cyprus (his grandparents) settle into a life of racism and violence, familial and social abuse in the UK. There is little in the way of a cup of tea offered. 'There Are No Ends, Only Intervals' begins with a description of violent racist bullying, then moves into an intimate space with a girl called 'Chloe', where the speaker remains an outsider. The girl's conclusion to his problems is to kiss him:

> the only way to speak to a person who hurts
> is to kiss them enough their mouth learns
> how to salvage love from spit on the floor

This is a comforting but ultimately superficial solution, one that the poem admits goes nowhere as it develops into further violence and the speaker ends up beaten at home 'for smoking'. An interval fades into another interval, the conclusions slight, the events matter of fact.

All of Anaxagorou's strongest poems develop out of occasions directly connected to his life; his witnessing ('Testimony as Omission'), his masculinity and girls ('Cocaine God'), violent encounters with his father ('How Men Will Remember Their Fathers'), bullying because his skin is darker ('After the Formalities'), his relationship with his own son ('Sublimation'). As the book moves forward, poems about friends and others are less distinct. 'Meeting the End of the World as Yourself' is a catalogue of vagaries that fails to be anything except vague. I'm not certain what 'What the Lesser Water Boatman Had to Say' has to say. More problematically, the language in his poems often progresses in an encumbering way, clear at first and growing more and more dense:

> the blackest red I'd ever seen his brother
> gripped her as she spun like a Cold War fan
> all of us then that boy her son his brother
> hated tomorrow left us sucking vinegar
> from two grey feathers to his heaven
> I came with the closing circle to name.
> ('Unpronounceable Circle')

What is a 'Cold War fan'? A Cold-War era mechanical contraption for swishing the air around? A pun, the fan as in fanatic? We start to see the image, but then as quickly wonder what the 'Cold War' has to do with it. And how does one suck vinegar from a grey feather? Do only grey feathers have vinegar? Then there's this, also from 'There Are No Ends, Only Intervals':

> ...my father the logician hit me too hard
> his eyes two charged weevils his willingness canine
> knuckles of expired milk the door locked my mother
> away on her knees begging his rage to keep me alive

Weevils are commonly found in dry food goods gone bad. 'Expired milk' is not the same as soured milk; it may yet be drinkable. The imagery wants to take us to the rotten, to the inedible/undrinkable, but doesn't really, partially because of that 'canine' hanging there at the end of the line, which suggests consumption and ferocity. Are these mixed metaphors the speaker's point? Is the language

out of control on purpose? It's difficult to tell if there is something here or the images are red herrings. We can forgive a few red herrings in a debut, but not the confusions these bring us to – even if Anaxagorou's message is clear.

Carnivores

Nicholas Friedman, *Petty Theft* (Criterion Books), $22

Reviewed by IAN POPLE

Nicholas Friedman is a natural storyteller. Each of the poems in this, his first collection, has a satisfactory trajectory. And this is not to say that the poems are too neat, or so constructed as to be airless. But there is a real sense of rest at the end of each poem. In addition, to that control of trajectory, Friedman is a very fine traditional technician. The forms range from rhymed quatrains to unrhymed sonnets, to pentameters, which Friedman handles with considerable aplomb.

The blurb for the book remarks on the title, commenting that the poems often depict loss. And that is true up to a point. But Friedman tends to choose subjects that have a quality of isolation about them. He is drawn to circus performers through the ages. An early poem in the book 'The Outlaws of Missouri, 1883 commemorates the brothers, Ford, Bob and Charley. Bob is 'the man who shot The Outlaw Jesse James', as in the film with Brad Pitt and Casey Affleck. A year later, the two men are part of a sideshow, and finally the shooting of Bob Ford, too. Friedman's sympathy is clearly with the two men who have now achieved an unwanted notoriety, which has lead, in their case, to addiction to laudanum. Later, Friedman writes about 'Tiny Tina' who 'at two-foot-five, she's queen of county fairs,' trading on the description of her show as 'Proudly ALIVE and EDUCATIONAL.' The poem ends 'a cul-de-sac of footprints when she goes'.

Friedman chooses these performers as exemplars of the way that humanity seizes on discomfort to establish comfort; that normality is established by establishing the opposite. Friedman's poems look at this sidelong. His position is not quite to send these things up; Friedman's own empathies attest to the complexity of these opposites. At the end of the poem 'Compulsion' with its subtitle 'at the Texas Prison Museum, Huntsville', the narrator sits down to eat and his companion, noting the opposition to the death penalty, comments, '"Burning the flag for evil murderers – / can you believe that? They're such *nasty* people." / He eats his plate of meat. And I eat mine.' That final line with its emphatic row of monosyllables underlines the way that Friedman creates his oppositions. This is emphatic but with its simplicity, the line opens the final judgement for the reader. The narrator, the 'I', is judged as well as the 'he', even as the 'I' has the final word.

This is such a well-orchestrated first book that it will be interesting to see Friedman's career from this point on.

Duck Three Ways

Jenny Bornholdt, *Lost and Somewhere Else* (Victoria University Press) $25

Reviewed by MAITREYABANDHU

What do we expect from a poem? Not much, judging by the paucity of serious poetry readers (as opposed to Instagram liker and trend-followers). It was Michael Donaghy, I think, who said that reading a poem was like meeting a stranger at a party. What he wanted from both was good company: rapport, engaging conversation, a laugh. No-one wants to be buttonholed by a religious bore, an over-earnest liberal or a ranting politician. Reading New Zealand poet Jenny Bornholdt's *Selected Poems* (in sumptuous UVP hardback) I met a woman I'd like to bump into at a party or sit next to on a train. She is excellent company: unpretentious, witty, moving, and, for the most part, short. Her poems talk about a world that those of us fortunate enough to be able to buy a book of poetry can recognise, in a way that gives it a little corona of light.

A reader new to Bornholdt's work could do no better than start with her 2008 collection *The Rocky Shore*, effectively a book-length autobiographical poem where humour, everydayness, love and pain – her father's death, its effect on her sons, her health problems – mingle and mix. I'd call it a major achievement if that didn't sound so terribly grand next to lines so seemingly casual.

The two questions that interested W.H. Auden about a poem were firstly the technical question of 'Here is a verbal contraption. How does it work?' and, secondly, the broadly moral question of 'What kind of guy inhabits this poem? What is his notion of the good life and the good place?'. Reading Jenny Bornholdt's new collection *Lost and Somewhere Else*, the answer to Auden's first question is: her poems are mostly written in short free-verse lines that aim at the 'casual perfect', the apparently off the cuff, the I'm-not-really-trying. The answer to the second question – what kind of 'guy' inhabits the poems? – takes us to the heart of what's so good about her work.

Bornholdt's notion of 'the good life' is family life: sons and sisters, a father's dying, a husband she loves (the writer, poet and painter Gregory O'Brien). Her 'good place' is New Zealand, especially as evidenced by her back garden, seen from her kitchen window, or written about in her garden shed. It's the domestic sublime with the gas turned right down. Many people, too many, write in this vein. What we usually get is the feel-good epiphany, the wouldn't-it-be-nice-if-we-were-nice. With Bornholdt we get something integral: Marianne Moore's 'a place for the genuine'. It's hard to think of a poet further removed from the grandiloquence of Wallace Stevens and yet when, in 'An Ordinary Evening in New Haven' Stevens says 'The serious reflection is composed / Neither of comic nor tragic but of the commonplace' we come back to Bornholdt's warmth; her unfussy, serious concern:

Boys turn into men
go out late and forget

to come home again
('Almost Haiku')

Bornholdt's new collection clarifies concerns that run through her work: the everyday, marital love, family, the lemon tree in the garden. Concerns shot-through, sweetened almost, by mutability and loss. The home territory of poetry. What makes the 'kind of guy' who inhabits these poems so worth meeting is the good-natured sanity, a kind of luminous sanity, that shines through them:

Let's eat duck
three ways. The first
the way my flatmate hit one
in his car. After bundling the body
into the boot, he
drove home, traumatised,
to tell us. Opened
the boot
and out it flew.
('Duck Three Ways')

Glad to see you coming / Hard to see you go

Tess Gallagher, *Is, Not Is* (Bloodaxe) £12

Reviewed by DAVID C. WARD

There's always something creative about the edge, the margins, and frontiers. Dividing lines where one can perch, in but not completely of one side or the other, and take stock on both people and past time. The poet Tess Gallagher divides her time between the American Northwest and the north-western coast of Ireland near Sligo. The dual locales provide her with subject matter and topics – whales in the Pacific; abortion politics in Ireland – but marginality is as much a cast of mind as it is a place. Most poets have it to begin with – the sense of looking slant – and the real distance in Gallagher's poems is between herself and her past, especially from those she has lost. Gallagher is rooted in Port Angeles, Washington and Sligo now by the graves of her husband poet and writer Raymond Carver and her long term companion, artist Josie Gray. Her title 'Is, Is not' gestures to death's sleight of hand: you're here; now you're gone. What are we to make of that dividing line? That absence?

What Gallagher has made of it is a series of elegies and reflections on her personal history, both family and friends. Raymond Carver could write brutally about American poverty and its effects. Gallagher is a little softer but you can still get a sense of how hard a hardscrabble life can be. Her coal miner father tells of the 'hell life' in the mines, asking 'How could a child lift that?'. But, lessons were learned:

One message mapped our days – *do
without!* It must be coded into my DNA
through a long line of chancers,
scavengers, people living on the edge.

Doing without makes you resourceful, turns detritus into something useful, even a poem: 'if something breaks or you think you've used it up – think again!'. Think again: a nice doubleness as you repurpose the details of your life but also think back again about it and re-cast it. Gallagher's poem 'What Does it Say' is about the only shoe repairman in town retiring, making that retirement into the passing of the sociability of the older artisanal crafts and economy. The man who repairs what we've worn out: 'a man true / to this gradually / falling-apart era, alive / to our need to be treated / mercifully, our wish / to be mended and remended?'

Many of these poems are dedicated as mementos to family and friends, or to their memory, and go from a specific instance to a more generalized, and abstract, summing up. They're not morbid or lachrymose but the poems are aware of our mortality; they test its limits, and offer up a remembrance that balances between the two worlds. Aging and mortality is present in Josie Gray's stroke or the bypass and plastic heart valve of a friend, but not really dwelled on explicitly. Instead, Gallagher is storing up memories pre-emptively against imminent loss. Keanu Reeves, of all people, was recently asked on late night television what he thought happened when people died. His simple response (I think everyone was expecting some Hollywood new age gibberish) was: 'I think that when you die, the people who loved you will miss you.' Gallagher's poems eloquently fulfil this function, tallying her own life and capturing the connections. Some of her poems are sentimental: 'It is always warm where she is – a condition of heart.' But most are not:

No, let's store
your presence in our blood and breath
so when we step, you step and we never

get to any future which puts even one of us
out of sight.

The Larkin Project

Clive James, *Somewhere Becoming Rain: Collected Writings on Philip Larkin* (Picador), £12.99

Reviewed by MARTIN CASELEY

This modest collection collates all of Clive James' engagements with Philip Larkin, the man and the poetry. It is also, it becomes clear, a project to rehabilitate the latter from the problematic traits of the former. The earliest pieces collected here, published during Larkin's lifetime, are fairly straightforward appreciations, albeit spiced with customary Jamesian humour and witty phrasing. The review-essay 'Wolves of Memory', for instance, on the appearance of *High Windows* in 1974, notes that what that volume was really about was 'clarifying' Larkin's poetry, rather then developing it. More arguable, perhaps, is James' assertion that this collection was 'the peer of the previous two mature collections'. Can this view really be maintained, considering those two previous collections were *The Less Deceived* and *The Whitsun Weddings?* The notion that Larkin deepens his themes in this volume is, however, worth considering carefully: as James says, 'there is a connection between the circumscription and the poetic intensity.'

Over the years since Larkin's death in 1985, his carefully winnowed poetic corpus has been compromised and even overshadowed by revelations of alleged racist attitudes, the publication of collections of existing letters, plays about his romantic entanglements, even the discovery of spicy lesbian narratives – all of which makes writing about just the poetry rather more tricky than it once was. The character of 'Philip Larkin' has been moving dangerously close to the centre of the stage, a location totally alien to the man himself, by all accounts. James has plenty to say about the sequencing of Larkin's unpublished poems in the first posthumous *Collected Poems* of 1988, the value of his jazz criticism and the revelations hidden in plain sight in his letters to Eva, his mother. He also makes valiant efforts to explain Larkin's characteristic approach to American readers – probably a non-starter, but courageous, nevertheless, given the throbbing bass-note of repressed Englishness throughout his work.

Seasoned readers of Larkin's work will find plenty to stimulate them in some of James's verdicts. He values Larkin highly – higher than Eliot – and praises his discriminating eye, even at the level of syntax: one reason why he remains so quotable. He is also seen by James as a poet for all stages of a reader's life: we begin the journey by nodding along to the qualifications of 'Church Going' and end confronted by 'The Old Fools' and 'Aubade'. James gets this, and can explain it with precision, although I would have liked him to say more about key poems like 'The Explosion' and 'An Arundel Tomb', rather than spending so much time mounting a defence of 'For Sidney Bechet' and Larkin's penchant for jazz, as evidence against ingrained racism.

Some of the controversies concerning Larkin's supposed private views have faded, while the poems survive, gathering lustre, as James' continued dialogues with them prove. The most interesting piece for *PN Review* readers will be 'Yeats v. Hardy in Davie's Larkin', a 1973 TLS review of Donald Davie's *Thomas Hardy and British Poetry*. James shows why the 'large, argued Yeatsian strophe' and the allied 'rhetorical majesty' are so crucial to poems like 'The Whitsun Weddings' and, contra Davie, concludes that 'Larkin's heritage is a combination of Hardy and Yeats'.

The final pieces included here are recent ones, dating from 2014 and 2018 respectively, showing that James, now himself staring mortality in the face, remains fiercely engaged by the poetry. 'Larkin's verbal dynamism still tears me to bits', he states and, returning to memories of his first reading of *The Less Deceived,* pays a final tribute to 'a little book that did so much to teach a generation how the next world happens here, where we live now'.

The publication of this little collection reasserts James as a stimulating, entertaining critic and may help focus attention back on the poems, which do not seem to be going away.

From Mexico to Bremen

Pura López Colomé, *Speaking in Song (Hearing and Forgetting)*, (transl.) Dan Bellm (Shearsman) £10.95; Michael Augustin, *A Certain Koslowski – The Director's Cut*, (transls) Sujata Bhatt & Margritt Lehbert (Arc) £9.99

Reviewed by ROSS COGAN

According to Robert Hass, the work of Pura López Colomé, one of Mexico's leading contemporary poets, is marked by an 'incandescent inwardness, of the kind that Marina Tsvetaeva said she found in the poems of Rilke'. I'm not convinced by the comparison to Rilke, but the mention of Tsvetaeva is serendipitous. Tsvetaeva is famously hard to translate, with her complex rhyme schemes, compressed syntax and dense metaphors. I wonder if the same isn't true of López Colomé.

What strikes you most about *Speaking in Song* is the aptness of the title, since many of these poems have been set to music. And you can see how well they would work as songs. The short lines – often only two or three words – are packed with internal rhymes and assonance, forcing you to slow down and savour every syllable. The English translations can fall flat by comparison.

Not that there's anything wrong with Dan Bellm's work, which is invariably competent and occasionally inspired. But the task is a stiff one. Forrest Gander, another translator of López Colomé, has noted that the 'hermetic quality' of her poetry makes it tough to translate, particularly when placed alongside the difficulty of deciphering Spanish pronouns, which allow for ambiguities hard to mirror in English. Add to this the complexity of translating a language rich in end-rhymes that allows rhyme-schemes to arise almost organically, into a 'rhyme-poor' one like English, and you have a challenge for the best translator. So, for example, a musical passage like:

no confundas
transparencia
con plumosas vastedades
destinadas a planear;
no confundas propicio
con ubicuo
quehacer sin sangre
del profeta literal

('Praying Mantis') becomes: 'don't mistake / transparence / for a feathered enormity/ made to soar; / don't confuse propitious / and ubiquitous / that bloodless task / of

literal-minded prophets' – an explosion in a theology department.

'Hermetic' is an apt description of López Colomé's poems, as there's something mystical and intensely subjective about them. She has herself talked about poetry's 'transformative power' – its ability to 'make us stretch… toward our possible realities', and to render us capable of 'absorbing permanent suffering, the common denominator of the human race'. Although she claims to have lost the Catholicism of her youth, her verse is still informed by religious sensibility, as in 'The Soul to the Body':

I raised your eyebrows
as you lay dying,
peeled back your eyes,
so beautiful,
their burst blood vessels
still brimming with my image

More often, though, the spiritual aspects are muted and López Colomé encourages us to pay closer attention to our physical sensations. 'Lip Reading by Mind Reading', for example, opens with this demand: 'Let's use a language of gestures / to act as if nothing exists, / trapping / breath / in front of the lips.'

This is poetry to dance to. Kick off your shoes, move the coffee table and swirl around as gracefully as you can while you recite. Only recite the Spanish versions first.

Michael Augustin is a significant figure in contemporary German poetry: the recipient of the Friedrich Hebbel and Kurt Magnus Prizes and director of an international literary festival, he works as a writer and broadcaster for Radio Bremen. *A Certain Koslowski – The Director's Cut* is an expanded issue of the 1992 edition – itself a translation by Margitt Lehbert of the 1987 German first edition. To Lehbert's 49 translations it adds a further twenty-three by respected international poet Sujata Bhatt, who is also Augustin's wife.

According to the cover these 'brief prose pieces' are 'laugh-out-loud funny'. Well, perhaps they are. Certainly reviews use that exact phrase. Personally they reminded me of the Pink Panther cartoons that used to be aired on Sunday evenings in the eighties, where the wordless feline would pursue some obscure but trivial goal only to find the world around him changing in surreal ways. For example, he might open a door only to find that the expected room had disappeared, to be replaced by a sheer drop, or that he now emerged on the ceiling. These pieces disconcert us through similarly shifting perspectives.

Here, for example, is 'Question and Answer', a snappy rehashing of the liar's paradox, in full:

'"Is it true," someone asks, "that regardless of what one asks you, one always receives a wrong answer?"
"That's right!" says Koslowski.'

The pieces loosely follow the life of the eponymous Koslowski, whose birth can be placed somewhere in central or eastern Europe, sometime in the 1920s. In some ways he is a mythical figure ('According to corroborating reports from the Polish cleaning lady and his mother, the infant Koslowski's first words were "more light"' –

'From His Childhood'); in others he is everyman ('At the tender age of barely fourteen, Koslowski discovered to his amazement that the consumption of several glasses of alcohol... resulted in a state of complete inebriation' – 'An Experiment on Himself'). We follow him as he fails to become a violinist, finds and loses love, unknowingly shares a table with James Joyce, sleepwalks, is repeatedly mistaken for someone else, fails in several suicide attempts, and exhibits his 'singular talent of botching the punchline of virtually every joke he tells'.

It's all amusing in a mildly disconcerting way. But what is the point? I think probably this:

> His almost lifelong search for truth has really been crowned by a nearly overwhelming lack of success. And yet, in the process, according to Koslowski, he discovered 'a wonderful, sparkling palette of the most enjoyable and intelligent lies', which, as he says, 'in the final analysis are what make life worth living'. ('Finding Truth')

A Certain Koslowski is a reminder of how much a plausible, three-dimensional life story can consist of absurdity and incoherence.

Itching Foot-soles & Winter Hooves

Genzō Sarashina, *Kotan Chronicles: Selected Poems 1928-43*, edited and translated by Nadine Willems (Isobar), £10

Reviewed by TIMOTHY HARRIS

This is a remarkable little volume with a remarkable story behind it. Nadine Willem is a lecturer in modern Japanese history, and while doing research into the history of exchanges between Japanese and European radical intellectuals before the Second World War, she discovered in a city library among the papers of the anarchist Sanshō Ishikawa some mimeographed poetry magazines to which Genzō Sarashina (1904-1985) had contributed. She was struck by Sarashina's poems because of the sharp-eyed and sympathetic way they described everyday life in eastern Hokkaido and the interactions between the indigenous Ainu and the mostly poor Japanese settlers, and she decided to translate them. She has also provided an extremely illuminating introduction.

Hokkaido is a prefecture which few Japanese people know about, unless they are from Hokkaido itself, for until comparatively recently it existed on the extreme verges, as it were, of Japanese history. The island only became important in the latter days of the Shogunate and in the Meiji Era because of the threat from Tsarist Russia, and it was in the Meiji Era that Japanese settlement started there in earnest.

So, Sarashina tends to be regarded in Japan as a poet only of regional interest, if he has been heard of at all. He was also one of a generation of left-wing writers who were silenced or near-silenced in the late twenties and thirties, and who never really recovered subsequently what audience they had for their poetry and novels before that time.

He was the son of Japanese settlers in Hokkaido; he farmed himself for a while there, and he also taught the children of a mainly Ainu village (*kotan*) before being dismissed for his allegedly subversive ideas. He knew life there from the inside and understood the situation both of the Ainu people, who were being forcibly fashioned into good citizens of the Japanese state, and of the Japanese settlers. His poems are mostly anecdotal, and based on actual events. This is not always a recipe for good poetry, but in Sarashina's hands it is. He has a wonderful eye for the importance of what to other eyes may seem trivial, as well as for telling detail. He shapes things economically and well. He is seldom sentimental, sermonising, or patronising. He sees his interlocutors, especially the children with their energy and directness, as individuals. The verse is colloquial and free, owing nothing to traditional Japanese poetry, apart from the acuteness of observation that informs some of the best of the latter.

Here's the first part of 'Poem for Sekko', in which the effect on Ainu lives of governmental restrictions on hunting deer and catching salmon and trout is brought home:

> For the first time in ages I was eating some *akiaji* salmon I'd been given
> > when Sekko walked in
>
> – Sensei, *so you don't know much about hard times, then?*
> – *There's plenty of this at the spawning grounds where you go, isn't there?*
> > – *No way!* HAPO *mama brings home only guts and bones and we have to*
> > > smoke those ready for winter
> > – *But if there's enough to smoke that's pretty good, isn't it?*
> > > – *Naah. We have to smoke all of it now if we want to eat in winter.*
>
> Fourth-grader Sekko knows what's not in any textbook
> The deep-down layers of life.

As well as being very colloquial, the original poems include some dialect words as well as onomatopoeic and Ainu words. These words are kept as they are in the translations, italicised in the case of dialect or onomatopoeia, in small capitals and in a different type-face in the case of Ainu, their meanings coming immediately after them as they appear. Also, as you can see from the above poem, direct speech is put in italics.

The translation as a whole works very well indeed, and has a splendid energy:

> The lake's warm enough for swimming now
> Who cares about end-of-term reports, the summer break starts
> > next week
> Cherries are turning black and gooseberries red

Sparrows come to the cherries in the playground, the kids puff
      out their cheeks
      Foot-soles are itching to go...

But it is not all anecdote and energy. There are tales told by old Ainu men, about bears, about relations with the 'Shamo' (Japanese), and a resolutely unsentimental account of a dying child and his dog. There is justified anger, as well as sorrow, and you feel the pressures of the political situation in which Sarashina was writing not only from what he explicitly says but from the blank spaces he left in poems for readers to intuit what he was unable safely to say (a practice used by a number of left-wing writers, and one that was eventually banned by an increasingly repressive government). The book ends on an elegiac note with poems from the 1943 collection *Songs of the Frozen Plain* that are laments for the destruction of the Ainu people and their way of life, the disappearance of their gods:

    Mountain   sharp shrill coughing fit
    KUNNE REK KAMUI night-crying owl-god   his voice cracked
    What's he saying now?
    He rests his head against the god of lingering fire
    He hears the sound of winter hooves galloping across
      the frozen plain

Don't Read Poetry

Reginald Gibbon, *How Poems Think* (Chicago), $25.00; Stephanie Burt, *Don't Read Poetry* (Basic), $17.99

Reviewed by
EDMUND PRESTWICH

How Poems Think is hard work to read and surely was for Gibbons to write but it's gripping and rewarding in proportion to its difficulty.

Despite the catchy title, this isn't a simplified instruction manual. Gibbons draws on wide reading in the poetry of several languages and on the work of boundary-pushing critical theorists. Although his book is a hybrid of different kinds ('part memoir, part report, part essay', says Robert von Hallberg on the cover) and focuses on different topics at different times, its threads are densely interwoven, and Gibbons expects the reader to keep hold of them while he works through ideas that he admits he sometimes finds difficult to define.

A main thread is the idea that 'the interesting thing for any poet ... is to open up one's own language to resources of poetic thinking from elsewhere'. In saying this Gibbons doesn't mean *ideas* from elsewhere but *ways*

of thinking which come more naturally in other languages than they do in English. To follow his argument we must not only be experienced readers of poetry in English but try to internalise radically different ways in which poems evolve in other languages. This is easy enough when we're dealing with the familiar contrast between the concreteness of English and the abstraction of French, though I found that quotations from Yves Bonnefoy's criticism sharpened my sense of the value of the French way. It becomes more difficult when Gibbons considers differences between poetic thought in English and Russian. He talks illuminatingly about ways in which Russian poets find stimulus in what we sometimes think of as the prison of rhyme. However, when he gets onto what he calls apophatic poetics I struggle to follow him and, not reading Russian, am frankly not able to evaluate his argument, though I find it stimulating to grapple with.

Throughout the book, Gibbons deepens our sense of what it means to talk of poetry as multi-layered. Explorations of sound patterning in George Herbert's 'Virtue' and Keats' 'Ode on Melancholy' or of syntax in C. K. Williams' 'My Mother's Lips' do this in essentially familiar ways, although with brilliant sensitivity and attentiveness. But such self-contained layering is only a beginning. Poems, for Gibbons, don't just think on their own, they think in conversation with other poems. One figure for this, borrowed from Mandelshtam, is that of the allusion as a cicada whose nature it is never to be quiet. Another, common in archaic and classical Greek poetry, is that of the poet as weaver. Gibbons' last four chapters present poems from different times and cultures, illustrating the often unconscious persistence of tropes and patterns already familiar in archaic Greek poetry, exploring figures for poetic creation in Pindar, Homer and other Greek authors, contrasting the Greek goal of weaving diverse materials together to create a harmonious new work with Ezra Pound's creation of unresolved tensions and dissonances. Here too there are fine close readings of individual passages and thought-provoking explorations both of the interplay of figures across poems, and of the implications of the figuration of male poets in terms of the feminine art of weaving (with a suggestion that Helen depicting battle-scenes on her loom 'is Homer's emblem of himself, for with words he is weaving scenes of the war').

Gibbons says that his book is meant as 'in part a poem gallery and in part an exploration of how the poems say what they say'. In both ways it will deepen readers' sense of the interrelatedness of all poetry, quicken their interest in areas they haven't explored and waken their minds to fresh ways of thinking about what they already know.

In contrast to *How Poems Think*, Stephanie Burt's *Don't Read Poetry* is explicitly designed for easy reading. It's a kind of instruction manual – subtitled 'A Book About How to Read Poems' – but not for Burt's own Harvard students. She writes that it's 'for people who found "Meditations in an Emergency" by Frank O'Hara after hearing it on *Mad Men* or Percy Bysshe Shelley's "Ozymandias" after binge-watching *Breaking Bad*. It's also for people, most of them younger than I am, who are getting into poetry by watching poets' performances, live or on You-Tube, or through their own and their friends' often very personal websites'. Clearly such people will be varied in age, interests, experience and educational level. The instability of Burt's language suggests her uncertainty about who her audience really is. Within a paragraph she'll go from the extreme simplicity of someone explaining something to a child at primary school to knowing slang, before relaxing into a slightly stilted, simplified academic mode. This is a persistent irritation.

Other problems arise from contradictions in the very nature of the enterprise. The notional scope is vast. Contemporary poets, mainly American and largely representing poetry of protest and exclusion, jostle with American forefathers and foremothers, with British poets going back through Chaucer to Anglo-Saxon riddles, with Catullus, Homer, the epic of Gilgamesh... Such material is scattered in chapters headed 'Feelings', 'Characters', 'Forms', 'Difficulty', 'Wisdom' and 'Community', taking us through a series of poetic types or issues arising in reading. This being a short book (large font and generous spacing make it so, despite the page count) discussions are very brief. This can have advantages. Burt is an experienced teacher and a highly intelligent, widely read critic. She seems to have a great range of material at her fingertips, as well as being a poet herself. Broad, basic points about different poetic kinds and purposes are clearly expressed. Well-chosen quotations make a lively anthology of radically different kinds of writing.

The problem is that it offers only very brief glimpses of each of the kinds it presents.

Although the title and subtitle suggest that the book will focus on individual poems rather than a general idea of Poetry, it's actually structured in a way that uses particular poems to illustrate general points. This wouldn't be a paradox if the exploration of these poems then went beyond such an illustrative function. However, brevity and the demand for expository clarity nearly always prevent that. What Burt gives is summary overviews angled to general points. Moreover, despite frequent protestations of deference to the reader's taste and judgement, the fundamental stance of talking down to people presumed not to know the poems or their contexts encourages dogmatic assertion. Careless slips like 'That's Henry Howard, Earl of Surrey, writing probably in the 1640's' or confusion of Fra Lippo Lippi with his son Filippino sit badly with the author's authoritative tone and make you wonder how reliable other information may be. Readings can be surprisingly off target, as when Burt says of Chidiock Tichbourne's 'Elegy', 'these balanced figures for worldly insignificance work almost equally well as a Christian prayer and as a model for other (say Buddhist) resignation'.

To conclude, this seems to me a book that falls between two stools. Burt is a highly able critic but the brief she's set herself here limits her ability to write in a way that will stimulate experienced readers of poetry. At the same time, her treatments are too rapid and glancing to give a solid grounding to the vaguely defined beginners she seems to be aiming at.

Nowhere Warm

André Naffis-Sahely, *The Other Side of Nowhere* (Rough Trade), £7.99; Ramona Herdman, *A Warm and Snouting Thing* (Emma), £6.50

Reviewed by RORY WATERMAN

One of the most pleasing things about writing these columns for *PN Review* is that I get to pick both my winners, and my focus. I've decided to concentrate this roundup on poets who have published one full-length book before turning to pamphlets – something I did myself. I quickly grew to feel a little constrained by my first book, because I'd started trying to do different things. Putting some of that into a pamphlet helped me to test out where I might be going, to grow. The two poets discussed below seem to have comparable motivations, and have certainly moved on with admirable assurance.

Few people are unrooted citizens of the world in the fashion of Andre Naffis-Sahely, whose first full-length collection was published in 2018. That forthright, erudite and absorbing book owes an occasionally slightly uneasy stylistic debt to Michael Hofmann, an enduring influence, and is called *The Promised Land: Poems from an Itinerant Life*. Naffis-Sahely was born in Italy, raised in the United Arab Emirates, educated in Scotland and England, and has now (or at least *for* now) settled in the western United States – where, if the poems in *The Other Side of Nowhere* are anything to go by, he does not seem to have found his Promised Land:

MAKE AMERICA GREAT AGAIN,
BUY REAL ESTATE! Hail follows rain.
Nearby, the township of Sunsites,
once billed as the safest

spot to survive
the inevitable nuclear winter,
actually topped Soviet Russia's
list of high-priority targets... Enter

the Orange Duck Candidate.
A haboob sweeps across
the Valley of the Senile.

This indicates much of how Naffis-Sahely's poems often tend to work, in broad terms. The ironies and tensions are thick yet tacit, the enjambments often positioned to emphasise them. His attention to detail, to resonance, is often exquisite: Sunsites is a real place (look it up on Google Earth and shudder), and of course one with a cheerily descriptive name that is, at least temporarily, a lie; the Valley of the Senile obviously isn't a real place, but one senses the poet thinks it should be. Decorum can go fuck itself. This reads quickly and easily, and superficially looks simple, but it isn't.

This little pamphlet is broken into three tiny sections, each a miniature sequence with its own internal energy. The first, in two parts, pulls us from the apparent wastes of a self-satisfied and perishing Arizona – 'the desert is human / endeavour's most fitting graveyard', he tells us, revealing his trademark sunny disposition – to the country in which his life began:

> Weeks ago, two cops in Catania
> stung a sixteen year old boy from Darfur
> with cattle-prods to impart the following lesson,
> *'whatever the government says,*
>
> *you're not welcome here.'*

The second section is in a very different gear, and comprises chipper elegies to American musicians and showmen, Gram Parsons and Arthur Lee – two figures on a different other side of nowhere:

> Sun-drunk, I roll
> along the streets of Los Angeles,
> while the radio rewrites
> the world as I know it.

Plenty of that world as he knows it has been summed up in the opening two poems; but these next two are paeans to escapism, albeit escapism of a very self-aware and temporary kind. Unfortunately, though, this section is a relatively weak middle movement, the final sentiment unmovingly pat: 'who could fail to remember you, / sweet, druggy prince of South Florida oranges?' Sure. So what?

The final section of five short poems, 'Forgotten Californians', is a bold return to form, and a sure sign that Naffis-Sahely hasn't rested on doing one sort of thing well. This 'sequence of found poems' shines sudden bursts of torchlight on a fragmented American past that might fruitfully be remembered, from the racist labour leader Denis Kearney, to the late-nineteenth-century Chinese-American activist Wang Chin Foo, to the reclusive and elusive John Samuelson (look him up) and, through him, essentially to the present and eternal, and the pamphlet's leitmotif: 'With time, the oceans grind the hardest / granite into sand... Nothing proven after death.' *The Other Side of Nowhere* is the work of a fine younger poet pushing himself, carefully and honestly. Few poetry pamphlets are this tight, tense, nuanced – or unresolving. He hasn't been noticed as much as he deserves to be.

*

Ramona Herdman, who lives in Norwich (that's all, folks), published her one full-length collection a long time ago now, in 2003, and she doesn't seem very proud of it. The biographical outline on her website contains only one flat and uninviting note on that book, telling us it 'is now out of print.' I have no idea what it is like, but the quality of her recent work implies that her judgement can be trusted. In recent years, she has published excellent pamphlets with HappenStance (*Bottle*, in 2017) and now with the Emma Press. *A Warm and Snouting Thing* is by turns funny, sad, mildly self-absorbed and self-criticising. The title comes from a poem here called 'There is a thing', which does a good job of summing up her endearing, vulnerable, strong-willed aesthetic (the title runs on in the first line):

> that's maybe me
> or maybe part of me. A warm
> and snouting thing that snuffles round
> at possibilities, that bounds
> across the fields alongside my commute,
> that one day really will
> abandon the train at Manningtree [...].

If that doesn't speak to you at all, this pamphlet will not be your bag. But Herdman is a poet who really notices things, and whose poems display an infectious zeal for life. There is nothing especially original in her subjects or concerns, but her writing is limpid and memorable. The opener 'He sits slightly too close and we don't look at each other' is essentially an exercise in finding the right image for a sexually-charged near-encounter:

> I'm humming with it. Not at all like
> an electric shock. Perhaps a bit
> like your naked tongue about to lick
> a battery. Quite like sudden sun
> through a window – dazzling one eye.
> Almost the same as standing stock-still
> as the bonfire's heat advances,
> feeling its breath start to hurt your face
> as you stare back, smoke in your throat.

There's a lot of sensual experience in this pamphlet, and a lot of striking imagery, though a few of the pieces are a little too pithy for their own good. However, Herdman can turn this objective clarity on weightier subjects, too:

> [...] mid-argument,
> pre-divorce, he'd strip off. He did it once
> in front of my mum's friends, making a point,
> his sad body like something from the zoo.

However, perhaps the most impressive trait on display here, in several poems, is Herdman's ability to make simple statements of fact resonate emotionally, as a result of the context in which she puts them. Vivid scene-setting suddenly and often movingly gives way to unceremonial pronouncements such as 'The two of them dead now', or 'My mother phones to say / walking's got difficult so she's decided to stop'. She can turn on the zeal but, like Naffis-Sahely, she knows how to let a situation speak for itself as well.

Sinéad Morrissey is the author of six collections, all published by Carcanet, and the recipient of both the T.S. Eliot Prize and the Forward Prize. She is Professor of Creative Writing at Newcastle University and Director of the Newcastle Centre for the Literary Arts. Her selected poems, *Found Architecture*, is published by Carcanet. He teaches Shakespeare in Sydney. **Mark Dow** is author of *Plain Talk Rising* (poems) and of *American Gulag: Inside US Immigration Prisons*. **Philip Terry** was born in Belfast, and is a poet and translator. He is currently translating Ice Age signs from the caves at Lascaux. *The Penguin Book of Oulipo*, which he edited, appeared in 2019. **John Robert Lee** is a Saint Lucian writer. His *Pierrot* (poems) is published by Peepal Tree in 2020. **David Rosenberg** lives in Miami, close to the Everglades ecosystem he has studied for a quarter century. His *A Life in a Poem* was published in 2019 by Shearsman. *A Poet's Bible* won the PEN America translation prize. He was a Guggenheim Fellow in 2013 and most recently a visiting professor in the creative writing department of Princeton University. **Maria Stepanova** is a poet, essayist and journalist. Her collection of poems *War of the Beasts and the Animals* is published in English by Bloodaxe this September, as well as her prose book *In Memory of Memory* (Fitzcarraldo). She is the founder and editor-in-chief of the online independent crowd-sourced Russian journal Colta.ru. Carcanet will publish **Bill Manhire**'s new collection, *Wow*, later this year. **Leeanne Quinn**'s second collection of poetry, *Some Lives*, will be published by Dedalus Press in 2020. Her first collection, *Before You*, was published in 2012. She lives in Munich, Germany. **James Womack** is the author of *Misprint* (2012) and *On Trust* (2017). He has translated poetry by Mayakovsky and Manuel Vilas; a new collection, *Homunculus*, is due later this year. **Ange Mlinko** lives in Gainesville, Florida. Her most recent book is *Distant Mandate* (FSG, 2017). **Jeffrey Meyers**, FRSL, has recently published *Robert Lowell in Love* and *The Mystery of the Real: Correspondence with Alex Colville in 2016, Resurrec-* tions: *Authors, Heroes – and a Spy* in 2018. **Tony Roberts**'s fifth Shoestring Press collection, *The Noir American & Other Poems*, was published in 2018. His second book of essays on poets, poetry and critics, *The Taste of My Mornings*, appeared in spring 2019. **Gwyneth Lewis** was Wales's National Poet from 2005–06. She wrote the words on the front of the Wales Millennium Centre. Her most recent publication is a translation, with Rowan Williams, of *The Book of Taliesin* (Penguin Classics, 2019). **David C. Ward** is Senior Historian emeritus at the National Portrait Gallery, Smithsonian Institution. His *Call Waiting* was published by Carcanet in 2014. **Martin Caseley**'s essays, articles and poems have appeared in *PN Review, Agenda* and *The Countryman*. He contributes reviews to the stride magazine website (www.stridemagazine.blogspot.com), to *International Times* and *Review 31*. He has recently written on Geoffrey Hill, Bob Dylan, hares, Ronnie Lane and Charles Wright, and lives in Norfolk. **Rory Waterman**'s second collection, *Sarajevo Roses*, was shortlisted for the Ledbury Forte Prize for second collections. His third, *Sweet Nothings*, is due from Carcanet in May. He is Senior Lecturer in English at Nottingham Trent University. **Hal Coase** is a playwright and poet. He completed an MA Creative Writing at the University of Manchester in 2018. He currently lives in Bologna. **Maitreyabandhu** has published three collections with Bloodaxe: *The Crumb Road* (2013), a Poetry Book Society Recommendation, *Yarn* (2015) and *After Cézanne* (2019). **Edmund Prestwich** grew up in South Africa. He taught English at the Manchester Grammar School for thirty-five years and has published two collections of poetry. **Timothy Harris** lives in Tokyo. Recent translations from the Japanese have appeared in SNOW (Lewes, UK). He is the editor of *This Great Stage of Fools: An anthology of uncollected writings by Alan Booth* (Bright Wave Media, Yokohama). **Ross Cogan** studied philosophy, gaining a Ph.D. A writer and editor, he has published three collections, *Stalin's Desk* and *The Book I Never Wrote*, with Oversteps and *Bragr* with Seren.

COLOPHON

Editors
Michael Schmidt
Andrew Latimer

Associate Editor
Charlotte Rowland

Design
Cover and Typesetting
by Andrew Latimer

Editorial address
The Editors at the address
on the right. Manuscripts
cannot be returned unless
accompanied by a stamped
addressed envelope or
international reply coupon.

Trade distributors
NBN International (orders)
10 Thornbury Road, PL6 7PP
orders@nbninternational.com

Represented by
Compass IPS Ltd
Great West House
Brentford, TW8 9DF, UK
sales@compassips.london

Copyright
© 2020 Poetry Nation Review
All rights reserved
ISBN 978-1-78410-831-1
ISSN 0144-7076

Subscriptions (6 issues)
INDIVIDUALS (print and digital):
£39.50; abroad £49
INSTITUTIONS (print only): £76;
abroad £90
INSTITUTIONS (digital):
subscriptions from Exact Editions
(https://shop.exacteditions.com/
gb/pn-review)
to: *PN Review*, Alliance House,
30 Cross Street, Manchester
M2 7AQ, UK

Supported by